L-Plates For A Teacher

Joan Park

LARGE PRINT
Oxford

First published in Great Britain 2006
by Isis Publishing Ltd.

Published in Large Print 2006 by ISIS Publishing Ltd.,
7 Centremead, Osney Mead, Oxford OX2 0ES
by arrangement with the author

British Library Cataloguing in Publication Data
Park, Joan
    L-plates for a teacher. – Large print ed.
    (Isis reminiscence series)
    1. Park, Joan – Anecdotes
    2. Teaching – Scotland – Glasgow – Anecdotes
    3. Teaching – England – Liverpool – Anecdotes
    4. Large type books
    I. Title
    371.1'02'092

ISBN 0–7531–9348–5 (hb)
ISBN 978–0–7531–9349–5 (pb)

Printed and bound in Great Britain by
T. J. International Ltd., Padstow, Cornwall

To my friends,
Joyce, Marie, Mary, Maud and others,
who shared my days at
"Limewood" and "Kingston".

INTRODUCTION

About forty years ago, after seven lessons at the local driving school, I put up the L-plates on my husband's new car and with him at my side I started up the engine, released the hand brake, neglected to look in the mirror (his words), engaged gear and slid to the bottom of our avenue. There I halted, looked in all directions and made a left hand turn into the hill which runs down into the main road. Halfway down the hill, as we approached the bend I hit the first lamppost. It was a new car and it cost seventy pounds to repair the damage, but undaunted I finished the fifteen-lesson driving course and then rested up so that the car would be whole for our annual summer holiday. During the spring of the next year a kind and patient male friend of my husband taught me, in the following order, how to stop a car, how to start it, how to listen to the engine, how to change gear and how to drive with care round a deserted block on an industrial estate on a Sunday. We did this for many Sundays and my confidence, if not my driving skills, flourished. I practised reversing, three-point turns and hill-starts and had it not been that we could only rendezvous about every third Sunday, practice might have made perfect. As it was, each lesson brought me just about as far as when the last one ended.

After some months, my good-tempered instructor suggested that the time had come to invite my husband to accompany us, the idea being that he should be so impressed with the improvement that he would be willing to act as my qualified co-driver for the short intensive spell prior to taking my driving test.

My husband did sit behind me the following Sunday and, as I started off from my home in a quiet avenue with not a vehicle in sight, he quietly commented, "No signals!" and I was back to square one, crashing the gears and aware only of my gross incompetence. To be fair to my husband, he did allow me to drive on several occasions after that but each time the unexpected happened I was slow to react. His final observation was, "Let's face it. You'll never be a good driver and in Glasgow traffic, if you're not a good driver you'll be a dead driver." That finished it as far as I was concerned. Since that day I have never again put up my L-plates. I try to convince myself that my failure should teach me something about myself. It is for this reason that I use it as an introduction to the chapters which follow, not because they are about me learning to drive but because they are about me learning how to teach. In the field of teaching I remain a learner but, as with the driving process, I have learned a good deal about myself.

On her first day at school, my sister was given plasticine. Her teacher, evidently not one of the "enlightened", told her to make a tree. I presume that my sister enjoyed the experience of handling the plasticine but when the teacher returned to her some time later all she saw was a neat sausage of plasticine.

"You haven't made anything," she said.

"Oh yes, I have" protested my sister.

"What have you made?"

"I've made a rolling pin."

"But why did you make a rolling pin when I told you to make a tree?"

"Because I wanted to," was the reply in the unvarnished, tactless truth.

I feel rather like my sister. What I am about to write will at times, I am sure, sound childish, arrogant, tactless and lacking in imagination. My only excuse for writing about my teaching experiences is, in the words of my sister, "Because I wanted to" and in my own, "Because it's true."

CHAPTER
ONE

I do not decide to enter the teaching profession from any sense of vocation. It is several quirks of fate which conspire to land me in a teacher training college.

It is September 1941. The war has been on for two years, during which time my fellow school-mates have, one by one, succumbed to the temptations of the world in the form of well-paid office jobs to tide them over until they are of age to seek adventure in one of the women's forces.

Having surveyed the seven remaining members of the sixth form with the cruel eye of seventeen summers and having decided that I am cast in a different mould, I too reject former thoughts of a teaching career and announce my intention of leaving school to seek my fortune in the field of journalism.

Possibly from a strong sense of vocation but more probably because the staff shortage is becoming acute and the subtraction of a potential eighth member of the sixth form might entail the displacement of one of her staff, the headmistress delivers her advice. "Journalism is such an insecure profession. What kind of position do you think you will have attained in one year when you will be eligible for call-up? You will probably still be making the tea for the office staff. Why not return to your original idea of teaching? You have much to gain from a sixth year at school and when you become qualified to teach you will only teach from nine to four each day, with twelve weeks holiday a year — plenty of time to find out whether or not you can write."

I cannot fail to see the logic of this proposal and I apply for admission to Liverpool teacher-training college. In the year I stay on at school in order to satisfy college age-entry requirements I follow the Higher syllabus for English, French, Biology and History, free from the need to sit examinations. I like to think that this is the one year of my school course in which I am taught little and perhaps learn most. I dare not be so presumptuous as to say I learn to think for myself, but I do learn that there is more than one way to think about everything.

I revel in the anti-authoritarian views of G. B. Shaw and H. G. Wells. I glory in the language of Shelley and Ruskin and Keats. Teachers come to us in our small den where we all sit round a table. They can easily be diverted from the set text to enter into discussion on our favourite topics of religion, politics and parents. As a group we continue to converse on these subjects and others in what are called our private study periods. When July arrives, it is with a sad heart that I say goodbye to the companions I had once thought so stuffy.

Lacking funds for a course of two-year study, it is the custom for students to apply to their local authority for a loan. Each student is ushered into a room where about a dozen members of the Corporation sit at a round table and the questions are fired from all directions. Once I am seated the first question almost paralyses me.

"Why do you want to teach?"

I resist the temptation to shock them by saying I am attracted by the thought of a pension at sixty. (As we waited for our interviews it had been agreed with much amusement that none of us were intending to teach for more than four years. As soon as the boys were demobbed we would be snapped up in the marriage market.) I mumble something about wanting to work with people and children being little people etc.

"How old are you?"

"I'm seventeen."

"You have to be eighteen to be accepted for training college."

"I will be eighteen in August. I understand the course begins in September."

"You sat your School Certificate examination a year ago. What subjects did you sit?"

I reel off the list: distinctions in English Literature and History, credits in English Language, Maths, Geography, Botany, Zoology, Religious Education and French.

"Are you fond of mathematics?"

"No."

"You'll have to teach it, you know."

"What have you been doing for the last year?"

"I have been following the Highers course for English, French, History and Biology."

"Why aren't you staying on to take Highers and go to university?"

"I don't want to specialise."

It is too difficult to try to explain that really I did want to go on to university but from my limited secondary school observation, the more one specialised in a subject, the narrower one became and I did not want to become dedicated to one subject to the exclusion of all else. The only young teacher on the staff who taught me, the only one who dressed in other than a hand-knitted suit and flat heels was a Mrs M. She taught Biology and having blushingly revealed the secrets of reproduction to us fifth-formers, by way of illustration left at the end of that term to have a baby. Maths was not my strong point but even I could work out that one in a staff of twenty was just five per cent, and that I should be one of the five per cent to survive among the dedicated was stretching the odds rather too far.

"With a training college diploma you will only be allowed to teach in Primary or Secondary Modern schools, you know."

"Yes, I do know that." I do not add that the very thought of teaching even ten-year-olds appals me.

"That's all for now. You'll be hearing from us."

Some time later I receive notification that I have been granted a loan of two hundred pounds, this sum with interest to be repaid over a period of five years when I start to earn a salary. I never see the money. It automatically pays my fees and residence for the next two years. One could say I attend college determined to get my money's worth. I think I do get value for money, but from 1944 to 1949 I frequently have to remind myself of this, as out of a meagre salary (starting salary is sixteen pounds a month) I pay back the loan plus interest to the tune of four pounds a month.

I am fortunate in that for the duration of my training St. Katherine's College is evacuated to Keswick, Cumberland. Here the students are billeted among several hostels where we sleep three and four to a room. For meals we make the compulsory trek to the Waverley Hotel in the main street. We do this in all weathers, sometimes for little more than a cold supper of spam and beetroot with a glass of water. On a rota basis we do the Sunday washing up. Lectures are held in the Keswick Hotel, the Co-operative Hall, a ramshackle hut on the Greta Bridge and two mansions on the outskirts of Keswick.

To my surprise I enjoy most of the lectures and classes and I learn to appreciate the long weekends when, packed lunches in hand, we walk for miles over the countryside, climbing Skiddaw and Scafell Pike and exploring Walpole country. A townee at heart, I envy the students who have a surplus of cash to spend lazing away an entire morning or afternoon in the milk bar or on an afternoon tea at Swindon Lodge and possibly the local cinema on a Saturday night. My poverty forces me into the full social life of the college and I find in companionship, conversation and fun much that is denied to the fewer plutocrats among our ranks. My only indulgence is a packet of Cooltipt cigarettes, jointly purchased and shared by three of us on special

Saturdays when we can invent some minor excuse for this celebration. Any pocket money I have is quickly swallowed up by the cost of files, file paper, art materials and other stationery needs. Set text books can usually be obtained at less than half price from our senior students. Those not available in this way I do without and hope they are in the college library. The sweet ration is spent on one two-ounce bar of chocolate per month.

Years later I will suffer the odd twinge of conscience as I provide my children with half-crowns to spend on bus fares and cafés. I will wonder whether I am depriving them of some essential character training and by what means I can secure for them a glimpse of the kind of entertainment which money cannot buy. With hindsight it is easy to see only the virtues of a wartime existence.

Poverty is not without its embarrassment. On one occasion I crash a borrowed bicycle on the Whinlatter pass and it takes me most of the year to pay by instalment the cost of its repair. To avoid laundry bills I pack my weekly wash into a small suitcase and carry it to the bus station whence, for the sum of one shilling, it is transported to the Liverpool bus station where my mother collects it. Are there no facilities for washing clothes in college? Such must be the case. Space is rationed, soap is rationed and even water is rationed. We are allowed one five-inch bath a week and sometimes the doubtful luxury of washing one's feet in the dregs of someone else's bath water.

College photographs reveal that I dress like a fourteen-year old schoolgirl, minus cosmetics, hair-dos, talcum powder, deodorants, foundation garments and the consequent poise which these luxuries afford. However, I am one of many who, never having known these feminine appendages, never at any time feel deprived. My father's clothing coupons provide me with men's pyjamas and a gabardine raincoat. Until I am twenty, the rest of my wardrobe consists of a pinafore skirt that was a present on my fourteenth birthday, school blouses and navy blue knickers.

Needlework is an essential part of the course. We have to spend our clothing coupons on materials to show our skills of cutting out, machining, hand-sewing and embroidery. I possess none of these skills and I have never used a sewing machine, but I decide to make a blouse and a set of panties and underslip, both of which are to be exhibited before inspectors. I manage to wear these for the rest of the war despite the bulkiness of the seams which I am far too scared to trim. There is not enough material to cut the panties on the cross as per the pattern, so they end up looking a bit like a pair of football shorts. In handwork, I learn to tat so I can edge the underset with lace and hope the inspectors will be so impressed by the hand-tatted lace that they will overlook the rest of my shortcomings. Further to impress, I knit a pair of Fair Isle gloves (more coupons for the wool).

Miss Gradditch (Granny Grad), in her rasping voice and odd turn of phrase, says, "I expect each student to produce a baby before the end of the year so she can exhibit a baby's layette." No-one in my year is willing to oblige.

Miss Taylor, whom we nickname Birdy Tweet, because with her long beak and her tiny mannerisms she so resembles a bird, is much more practical. Cotton thread by the spool is still unrationed. We learn to set up a loom and weave unwearable scarves in cotton. We learn to do knotting with macramé twine and produce belts. We gather the bits of fleece from hedges and stone walls, tease it, card it into rolags, spin it on handmade spindles, wash it, dye it and weave it into more unwearable scarves. These handcrafts are extremely time-consuming so the hostel sitting room is full of students plying these old-world crafts. Two American tourists, rare in wartime, are guilelessly admitted into what they think is a private hotel called Blencathra only to be confronted with this scene from the past. "How cute" is their polite comment.

I enjoy English and History lectures and we all have to attend Religious Instruction. Miss Williams, or Big Bill because she is huge in every way, teaches Old Testament and Arithmetic Method. At the close of the first Old Testament lecture, she beams and in her huge voice booms out, "In preparation for next week you will please read the first five books of the Old Testament." When we roll up for the first Arithmetic Method lecture she is covering the blackboard with all manner of calculations, none of which would appear to be correct. One of the Maths students eventually grasps that she is doing Spider Arithmetic or, as she is willing to explain, working to a base of eight. This is Big Bill's way of demonstrating the child's difficulty in apprehending that in the decimal system we work to a base of ten. I am baffled. Until that moment I had never realised it myself.

The fact that I enjoy lectures is wholly to the credit of my lecturers, not least Miss Clarkson, the lecturer in Education and Child Psychology who for me opens up new vistas of thought. From the beginning I find myself interested in the learning process. As she moves through each aspect of child development I mentally picture my eight-year old brother and recall him at his various stages so, instead of making copious notes while Miss Clarkson talks for an hour, I listen and in my notebook write something like "e.g. Frank and the ball of string" so I have very short notes to later revise.

I begin to realise that teaching is more than just a job. It is something that demands a deal of thought and planning and personality, and in these days I am very conscious of my ability to teach, given the chance. I will become far less confident of my ability when I do try to teach and at times will have to console myself with the thought expressed by a disillusioned male schoolteacher acquaintance who says, "Most teachers worry too much. Give the kids a bit of reading and a few sums. They're quite happy and you are earning your pay keeping them out of their mothers' way." If this is the reason why we teach, then accordingly I was about to earn my pay and in the process would be wasting plenty of time and energy in trying to do something more than that.

Oddly enough, the real hell of college is School Practice; the four-week period of each of the two years when, armed with all the technique, we go into battle in the schools and are defeated. Keswick School cannot house one hundred students, so we are farmed out to schools in Whitehaven, Workington and Carlisle. We travel daily by bus and the long journey over winding country roads is a nightmare for me. I spend the journey fighting off waves of nausea and it is with relief that I step off the bus but hardly in A1 condition to teach. Add to that a full day's teaching or observing, a stomach-churning lunch in a wartime British Restaurant, a return trip to college to arrive too late for tea, compulsory attendance at formal dinner, and working from eight in the evening until the early hours of the morning preparing lessons and writing up lesson notes, and the wonder is that we survive at all.

On my first school practice I teach in the Stanwyx district of Carlisle. The word "teach" has never been used so euphemistically. I have a class of bright seven-year old boys and girls, well-taught and well-disciplined. For me the only snag is that their elderly teacher is unwilling to abandon them to my supervision so, unless the college tutor is present, I take all my lessons with her sitting behind me at a high desk making sure that her pupils behave well. I dread to think how appalled she must be at my performance. I have no idea how much material to prepare for a twenty- to thirty-minute lesson and, as it seems to me, the worst of all possible horrors is to run short of facts and be unable to answer a child's question, I invariably prepare a term's work for a single lesson.

The geography lesson is one of my many disasters. The topic for the lesson is China. I spend an entire weekend reading up on China, its physical features, its climatic conditions, natural vegetation, population and religion. I talk for thirty minutes and it is doubtful whether I allow one single pupil question. The Buddha figure of the class teacher sitting behind me dares my pupils by so much as a fidget to give vent to their boredom. Some months later I observe a demonstration lesson given by a college tutor where, with a class of seven-year olds, she talks about a little Chinese boy in a certain area, his clothes, his meals, his home and the work of his family. There is even time in her lesson for the children to make their own illustrations of Chang.

My arithmetic lessons are no less of a disaster. I am so anxious to please the college tutor by including group activity that all my energies go into organising this and the aim of the lesson is never reached. Later I watch the class teacher, armed only with a piece of chalk, repair the damage. The pupils are with her every inch of the way, zealous in their answers, enjoying the difficulties which she presents to them and wildly enthusiastic to apply the rule for themselves. Active participation? She proves to me that this is essentially a mental rather than a physical activity.

It is a bit of an enigma that although this school practice only serves to show me my inadequacy, I emerge from it with unshattered confidence and enthusiasm. The kindness of my college tutor is responsible for this. She is very fair and her criticism is always constructive. When there is little else to praise she praises the effort I have put into the preparation. Each time she sees me teach, she praises what she calls my natural liaison with the children of that age group and commends my enthusiasm. I can see some slight justification for this praise in my approach to the extracts which I read to the class from *The Wind in the Willows*. As a pupil at school I loved to be given a part when we read aloud from *Julius Caesar* or *Twelfth Night*. More recently it was with no qualms that, at the request of the lecturer in Voice Production, I was the willing guinea pig who read aloud for the benefit of fellow students. Certainly I was embarrassed as both teacher and class listed all the indications of my Liverpool accent, but it would have taken more than that to discourage me.

It is rewarding to watch the reactions of the children to a well-told story. The seven-year old gasps in all the exciting pauses, laughs out loud, wriggles in his seat in enjoyment and gives his neighbour a knowing nudge when he anticipates what is about to happen in the story. At times the young headmaster comes in and squeezes into a desk beside one of the children. I know that his report will go to my tutor but I find it hard to think of him as a critic when he behaves as they do, joining in the gasps, the laughs, the wriggles and the nudges. I am doing something I can do well; something I believe to be worthwhile. In front of a child audience I am an uninhibited performer.

I am given senior pupils in my other two school practices so neither my innumerable failures nor my single success are to be repeated so memorably.

I do not have a class teacher sitting behind me, my classes do not disintegrate into chaos and fortunately for me a month is not long enough for the lack of teaching to become too apparent. In a short period following my departure from the school the class teacher will have rectified any damage I have done. At the end of my final year I pass all the required examinations and I am awarded a teaching grade which allows me apply to Liverpool for a teaching post.

At some point during these two years at college is planted an ideal; the ideal that it is my job as a teacher to help each child to fulfil the whole of his personality no matter how limited his resources; to instil in each child a love of learning for its own sake. It is a goal I will continue to strive towards all my working life. There will be times when it will become very dim, times when it will disappear completely and again times when it recovers. That is what this book is about; the pursuit of teaching by a perpetual learner. Training college does not turn out a skilled teacher. It merely equips an applicant with a form of Highway Code to get him started and perhaps, if he is lucky, some spark that keeps him going in the inevitable bad times.

CHAPTER
TWO

"We learn by our mistakes" is a trite phrase quoted by many, including those in the teaching profession, but it has become almost meaningless by its repetition. Nobody really believes it any more. We say it glibly after something has gone wrong which we thought we had planned so carefully that it would be perfect, or we say it when we have planned insufficiently and we are accepting the blame for the ultimate chaos.

How often as teachers or parents do we deliberately allow our children to make mistakes in order to learn? In the classroom there is in my opinion too much "Watch (or listen) carefully or you will make a mistake". Who can blame the child who begins to think that making a mistake is the worst sin of all? Better to crib an answer from a neighbour, better to submit an empty page, better to sit dumb than open your mouth and say the wrong thing. I am not trying to pretend that I am wholly innocent of such remarks and by all means we should encourage children to avoid careless mistakes, but genuine mistakes are surely to a teacher what a cough or a pain is to a doctor, a symptom of a maladjustment that is asking to be put right. If we are really teaching, should we not sometimes be contriving situations which allow children to make mistakes so that we may learn what is needing to be taught?

If this principle is a just one and children be deliberately allowed to make mistakes, then we might consider extending the principle to teachers in training. I am sure that in many schools accepting probationary teachers fresh from college there is a welcome waiting for the new life-blood of ideas and inspiration, even supposing that the more experienced teacher who receives a class straight from the hands of that probationer finds she has much leeway to make up.

I plead for the probationer teacher to be permitted to make mistakes; to try out all his new ideas and to find out for himself what does not work. I make this plea because I spend my probationary year in a school where no-one, neither child nor teacher, is allowed to make a mistake; where any original idea is strangled at birth by the stern disapproval which parades itself under the guise of experience and all, may I hasten to add, from the most worthy motives.

In the 1930s, when I was ten years old, I lived in the suburbs of Liverpool in part of a large housing scheme in which was eventually built a modern primary school. I say "eventually" because some people had been in the houses for over a year before the school was built and there being no school, there could be no enforcement of the law which decreed that parents must provide education for their children. My mother, never one to be governed by the mere letter of the law, sent her children on a tram to a school some three miles away so that there should be no gap in their education, but in that district there were not many parents like my mother.

When the new school opened I was a bit of a phenomenon and I suspect more of a nuisance than anything else sitting in the top class. In Arithmetic all the ten-year olds had to relearn from their two times table upwards, whereas I was smug in my ability to do fractions and decimals. It solved the teacher's problem of setting and marking separate work if I was sent messages, and I became the school messenger, top girl and head-teacher's pet rolled into one. I loved it but my mother, no doubt finding my pride in my newly found status insufferable at home, called on the head teacher to stress the fact that she did not approve of my skivvying. I admire that head teacher. In the throes of starting a new school in a new community, in the throes of staffing, stock and other problems, she yet found time in the privacy of her room to teach me for an hour each day. During that hour she set work for me to do at home and on the following day went over it with me. Her standards were high. "What! Ten years old and never read *David Copperfield*!" She poured facts into me as one might into a computer and I, robot-fashion, produced the correct answers to the set questions.

As a result of her efforts, I sat and passed what was then called the Junior City Scholarship and because I was her first successful pupil in her school, the first feather in her cap, I became from that moment her protégée. With interest she followed my mediocre secondary school career and toward the end of my final

20

year at college she wrote to inform me that she had requested Liverpool Education Authority to place me as a probationer in her school.

I remember plucking up my courage to reply, suggesting to her that as most of her staff remembered me as a pupil and as my home was but five minutes distant from the school where the children of the district knew me on Christian name terms, it was not a good idea. She replied in the words of Shakespeare, "There is a divinity that shapes our ends, rough-hew them how we will". To be fair, I really think she justified her actions to herself by her strong belief in the divine right of Miss G. In September 1944 I begin teaching in her school.

She arranges an appointment for me to visit the school before the close of the summer term and passes on to me copies of the set schemes of work for class 1A. I spend most of my summer holiday drawing pictures and charts and planning work for the seven-year olds. I have them for a week in September with Miss G. popping in at regular intervals to vet my performance. At the end of the week it has been decided that left to me the class would not benefit and I am transferred to make a mess of 2B. I think if I am allowed to make a mess of 2B without the constant criticism of Miss G., I may welcome the move.

The one piece of advice I receive from Miss M. with whom I am exchanging classes is, "Don't let them try anything on. If you're not careful they will never be in their seats. You've got a child on the front row, Edna Smith — she'll use any excuse to get your attention.

She'll be out at your desk the minute you set foot in the classroom, so even if she tells you that her mother died this morning just send her back to her seat." Thus armed I meet the girls of 2B who, with their various learning difficulties, have been made very conscious of their shortcomings.

An unwritten law decrees that they are expected to produce formal work to the same standard as their equivalent A group, but as it will take them longer to achieve this there will be less time allowed for creative work. The teacher is required to write everything on the blackboard which the class will copy into their notebooks. Even if the teacher rules by the rod and her pupils rewrite the exercise two or three times, there is but a slim chance that eventually each child might copy it correctly. I am frustrated, the class is frustrated and I teach nothing. I never even succeed in finding out what that class cannot do because we are all so busy setting things down on the right lines or the right boxes (the squares on the Arithmetic exercise books), with the right number of spaces in between. "Right" is dictated throughout the school.

I let the girls draw and paint the motifs for a composite wall picture. I help them paste their cut-out items on to the background painted in by their fellow pupils. Miss G. awards us a tolerant smile and directs me, "Look in Mrs B.'s room and you will see the kind of frieze which enhances the appearance of the classroom." On the recommended Autumn frieze, the background has been carefully drawn in by Mrs. B. and her best painters chosen to fill in the colours at her dictation. The rest of her class have drawn round templates to produce the trees, squirrels, rabbits and the rest which the teacher has later cut out carefully, thus making good any slip-shod painting, and all are stuck on in appropriate places. Arrogantly I judge that if this is the work of the top class, it demonstrates that in this area they have produced little more than might have been assembled by a class of seven-year olds.

The handwork scheme for my class (children who cannot hold a ruler straight or even make a crease in paper), as written in the holy script called Schemes of Work, is measuring: making envelopes and booklets correct to the eighth of one inch in paper or thin card. Timidly I suggest to Miss G. that I feel this scheme of work is unrewarding; the finished product takes so long to complete and is so inexpertly executed that the children feel little pride in it. "That," I am told by Miss G., "is the result of bad teaching." She will herself come in and take a lesson for my benefit.

I am to remember it vividly — forty children sitting bolt upright in their desks not moving a muscle until the order is given.

"Pick up your ruler in your left hand and your pencil in your right hand. Put the point of your pencil to the line on the ruler which marks the one inch. Hold your pencil there until I have walked to every desk to see if your pencil is in the correct place." She walks up the aisles to each desk in turn, commending or chastising as she deems fit, finally resuming her place facing the class.

"Lay your ruler to the edge of the paper. Put your pencil point at the place on the paper which the ruler shows is one inch from the edge. Hold it there while I see if you have done this correctly." Again she visits each desk and this process is repeated each time any mark has to be made on the paper. Some children become restless as their concentration wanes and their careless mistakes earn smacks which result in tears. In a thirty-minute lesson, each child has drawn one straight line. I dread to think how many weeks it will take to produce one grubby envelope.

If there was one subject I felt confident about teaching as I left college, it was Physical Education. In this I knew I had gained an A teaching grade and this not because I excelled in gymnastics, but because I could use my voice to make the children feel the kind of response I wanted: quick or slow, strong or light, strenuous or gentle. P.E. at this time was just and only just emerging from its long "soldiers on parade" stage, while we were trained that each lesson needed to contain some free activity, some group use of apparatus and some teacher-directed exercise.

2B enjoy their PE lessons and so do I, but it is short-lived. One day as my class run into the hall to collect their apparatus for free play, all instruction for this introduction having been given before we left the classroom, Miss G. follows swiftly at our heels to demand why I have lost control. I deny this and in order to demonstrate I command "Stop. Apparatus down. Find a space anywhere in the hall facing me." I am about to continue but authority takes over with a whistle (not a piece of equipment allowed for indoor PE) and the command, "March to your team lines immediately as you have been taught to do. Next time you enter the hall I expect to see you march into your team lines and stand to attention until your teacher tells you what to do. Don't ever let me see this bad behaviour again." Then, turning to me, "Miss Lowe, I will make arrangements for you to attend one of Mrs. B's PE lessons so in future you will know how it should be taught." I burn with resentment and some days later, as I sit through Mrs. B's lesson, I am still nursing my fury. Under the pretence of taking notes I soothe my injured pride by adopting the role of a PE inspector and writing scathing comments: "Where is the activity in this lesson? What is the teaching point of this exercise? Some of the children are arm-circling in a forward direction, why do you give no correction? Most of the children spend their group activity waiting for a turn!" Nobody else ever sees these comments and I go home and weep.

I suffer yet another defeat at the battle of Spelling. Anyone who, with a class, has had to make the change from script to the old cursive writing knows that this takes many hours of precious time. When pupils are able to concentrate fully on the writing they manage fairly well. When it is used in combination with the teaching of another subject such as spelling, the written result becomes a combination of script and cursive. In an effort to help my less than gifted class overcome this difficulty I say, "Now, until we have fully grasped the cursive writing, when you are writing from memory as in spelling or dictation we will stick to the script." It may not be the best way but having given it considerable thought it seems to be the fairest and least discouraging way.

One day Miss G informs me that she will be taking over my class for the final hour of the morning session in order to give a written spelling test, so I may use this time for marking or preparation in the staff-room. I regret the test being administered in the last period of the morning when concentration is flagging, but confident that we have really slogged at the spelling I leave my class to its fate. Anticipating the lunchtime bell, I am dutifully waiting outside the classroom door to supervise the dismissal of my class. In the corridor I am confronted with Miss G., her face a wrathful shade of red. Thrusting a pile of test papers at me she demands to know what I have been doing in the periods allocated to spelling. Glancing at the papers, I see she has insisted on them being executed in the cursive style. I point out to her that most of the "errors" are errors of writing not spelling and I try to explain how this has happened. She refuses to listen to what she calls my excuses. I am a hopeless teacher, I have put no thought into my preparation, there is only one way to teach spelling . . . I feel such a sense of injustice that when at last she pauses I cannot even speak coherently so my defence is useless.

Her tirade eats up precious minutes of the lunch hour that I had hoped to spend at home. I choke down my lunch to get back to school as soon as I can to get work written up on the blackboard so I shall not be accused of being ill-prepared again that day. As I decide to skip the after-lunch cup of tea, my mother pushes me back in the chair and from her handbag produces a packet of cigarettes. My mother is not a smoker. She carries the same packet of cigarettes in her handbag for a year for special occasions like an interval coffee at the theatre, a long train journey or to chase away the gnats at a picnic.

"If you can't learn to relax," she says firmly, "you are going to be ill. If you can't keep your eyes off the clock, you will never learn to relax. Now, it takes ten minutes to smoke a cigarette and, knowing that, you can take your eyes off the clock and when the cigarette is finished you can go back to school." Little does my mother suspect at the time that she is introducing me to a life addiction, but I think that even guessing that I could proceed from nicotine to heroin she might still have considered it the lesser evil.

If unwittingly my mother has set me on the road to corruption in 1944, smoking is at this time my single indulgence in the pomp and pleasure of this wicked world. I am nearly twenty-one and there is in existence a tolerant boyfriend called Brian. He works on a local paper and because among other tasks he reviews new releases at the local cinema, I occasionally find myself sitting in a free seat in the front row of the circle. More often than not he accepts my explanation that I have not time to go out and contents himself with underlining spelling errors, making weather charts, reading out marks for me to record and feeling one of the family. His parents lead separate lives though sharing the same house so, even cluttered with school books, my home is preferable to his own. Brian comes and goes and most of the time he goes and I am so irritable that the wonder is he comes at all.

My life is as narrow as a hermit's although my goal is different. My goal is to endure my world as it is for just one year. "Oh, God," I pray every night, "That is another day over. Make the hell of my existence pass quickly."

There is no fellowship in this school. If there is any camaraderie among the staff I do not share it. I am the probationer teacher but I think I fared better as the pet pupil. I still skivvy for the rest of the staff. The probationer does not share interval tea in the staff-room. It is her lot to patrol the playground, even on Fridays when they have a cake with their tea. Life might be sweeter if I could throw myself into some activity outside of school, but my confidence in myself has never been weaker and I am too scared of what Miss G. could say if she heard I played tennis or was a member of an amateur drama group.

"Many students straight from college take up all kinds of pursuits" is the theme of many such of her pronouncements, "If you want to be a good teacher, you have not time for anything but preparing your lessons so don't be taking up with time-wasting nonsense." She doesn't need to worry. From my narrow little world I never even realise that I have nothing to communicate even to my class.

It is the summer of 1944 when I begin teaching. One glorious September day I am taken to task for wearing leg make-up instead of stockings. I conduct my defence on the grounds that I have no spare clothing coupons for stockings,

"Nonsense," is the reply, "How is it that all the other members of staff have coupons for stockings?" I reply as politely as I can that while I have been out-growing my gym-slip, they have already accumulated a wardrobe of sorts which is standing them in good stead, so they can afford the coupons for stockings. I refrain from adding that, from my observations, these particular staff members have been hoarding their fashions since the turn of the century. My explanation, a very true one, cuts no ice. From Miss G's viewpoint, the stockingless legs are just further evidence that I lack the dignity of my profession. She is right. For this year I never willingly admit in public that I am a teacher. Inwardly I vow that if the staff of this school are teachers, then never will I confess to being of their like. Yet for all this I still have faith that if I can only get out of this particular school, I could enjoy teaching. The question is how to get out.

As Christmas draws near, possibly because I am now clad in stockings, possibly because I am, for the sake of peace, offering little resistance, there is a lull in the battle. My spirits soar when I am told that I may attempt to produce a play with my class for the Christmas concert. Of the arts, drama is my first love and as a child I had loved taking part in plays. Once I had even played one of the Ugly Sisters in *Cinderella* when I was a ten-year old in the class of Miss B., the now Mrs B, of this school. Perhaps Miss G. remembers this but I am inclined to think the assignment is one of convenience. Mrs B. now rehearses a choir, Miss M. plays the fiddle to accompany her dancing pupils, Miss C. produces a fairy tale in music and mime and, rather than have me poaching on their territorial reserves, it is decided that my effort should take the form of a straight play of *Rumpelstiltskin*, the aim to be clarity of speech.

I am given copies of the printed play and told to cast it. This I do. There are only speaking parts for about six characters but the children are interested and over a period of weeks we have the speech perfect, the moves reasonable and we have trained understudies for each actress. I beg few ideas from the children but rather impose my ideas on them and they are receptive, mimicking my phrasing, tones and actions. The one exception to these carbon copies of me is Maureen Kettlewell, one of the two girls who is acting the part of the miller's daughter, later to become the queen. Maureen has ideas of her own because she loses herself in the part and this has an advantageous effect on the rest of the cast. By contrast, Jean, who has also become practised in the same part, is wooden.

Miss G. attends the final rehearsals, for hers is to be the decision as to who should be allowed to play the part in the concert. Miss G. insists that Jean rather than Maureen will better fit the bill. Jean, in Miss G.'s words, is the prettier child, comes from a better home and is therefore well-mannered and Jean's mother will be disappointed if she is not chosen. So Maureen acts in the performance we give for the school and Jean acts for the parents. Later Miss G. admits not that she was wrong in her choice but that it could not have been anticipated that Maureen, so very backward in her schoolwork, could have carried out her part so well. I am complimented on my effort and I wallow in this rare praise.

I think it is as the result of the play that one day Miss G. takes me into her confidence sufficiently to tell me that although Liverpool Education Authority make it a practice to remove a probationer at the end of one year's service, she feels that my case is a special one and she is confident that she can convince the powers that be to agree. Apparently I have shown great improvement since my arrival and it is her firm belief that granted another year of her guidance I will make a good teacher.

"God help me," I think, "What you think of as my salvation will mean the destruction of my soul!" but it needs a stronger heart than mine to upset the Svengali relationship which I am finding preferable to the fray which has persisted so furiously for so long. Fortunately for me, within a week or two, while I am still trying to force myself to be open with my headmistress expressing my misgivings and risking her disfavour, we have a visitor to the school on a rare day when Miss G. is not in attendance.

It is after three in the afternoon and I am taking my wretched handwork lesson. In answer to the knock on the glass-panelled classroom door I look up to see a face I recognise, yet its very familiarity seems so out of place in this environment that I cannot put a name to the face. The person inclines her head to one side and smiles, a very gentle smile full of quiet dignity and sympathy, and suddenly, with a rush of emotion which brings a burning sensation to my throat and tears pricking at my eyes, I realise that here in these alien surroundings is the embodiment of all my adolescent ideals about teaching. It is Miss Clarkson, the lecturer in Education and Psychology who at college had so inspired me to want to teach. I make no apology for what must seem my over-dramatization of this reunion because for me it will remain treasured in my memory. When she quietly opens the door and asks my permission to enter the classroom it is the first time since I entered this building that I feel other than a pupil.

Requesting my permission once again she addresses the children while her eyes dart hither and thither taking in everything. Then with great perspicacity, it seems to me she inclines her head in her habitual attitude of asking a question and says, "This is a very beautiful, modern building, you'll agree? You have splendid classrooms and equipment, yes?" Then, lowering her voice to a whisper, "But I do not think you are very happy here?"

I dare not trust myself to speak but I shake my head and, tactfully she talks of other matters until I have regained my composure, then she continues, "I have been told that your headmistress is seeking to retain your services for another year? You must not allow that. You must go to another school."

I do not have to tell her anything about my miserable experiences. She has guessed all. With the minimum number of words she has established communication and, realising that she has done this, her mission is complete and just as quietly she leaves.

The next day I go to Miss G. and I tell her in a speech I have rehearsed through all the hours of darkness that, all things being considered, I do not agree with her that I would be better for another year at this same school and that I will be grateful if she will withdraw the application she has made on my behalf. She turns a slow purple at my lack of gratitude and assures me that, for my own good, she will not withdraw her request and if I insist on writing to the Education Authority myself to state my own immature opinions, I will only have myself to blame if I am transferred to the toughest school in Liverpool. I accept the challenge and, that evening, I write to the authorities. Carefully veiled in phrases such as "residing so close to the school", I state my reasons for wishing to transfer at the end of the summer term.

Fortunately for me I do not for long have to endure the consequences of my miscreant behaviour. To what extent I am responsible for Miss G. suffering a stroke which entails her absence for the remainder of the term, I will never know. It will be some years later when I hear that she never fully recovered.

The school continues to run on its despotic régime despite the absence of the dictator. As a staff we are all just as much her tools as if she had been present. Her slaves have lost the art of questioning authority even when it is no longer there. Like the ancient Israelites, we still obey the laws of Sinai but like them, too, we squabble among ourselves. I do not openly dispute the dictates of any member of staff. Most of them had taught me and I think of myself as one of the lesser brethren fit only for listening to the tales that each tells when another member's back is turned. I am counting the days to freedom.

CHAPTER
THREE

My enquiries about T.D. Wavertree School lead me to discover that it is situated a double bus journey from home in a declining area and I will be teaching Junior Mixed pupils. When on arrival I find it is housed in a building scheduled for demolition, that it contains three composite classes and that I am to be in charge of the top junior boys and girls, I appreciate that it is, in theory at least, the biggest contrast to my first school that I could hope for in the city of Liverpool.

To raise my already buoyant spirits, Miss Burton, the headmistress, appears, on first acquaintance, to be a placid, sad-faced, rather emaciated-looking little woman who, having had for some months the burden of teaching the upper juniors in addition to her duties as headmistress, is only too pleased to surrender them to me to do more or less as I please. With my youthful zeal and apparent good health I must seem to her, inexperienced as I am, like the arrival of the cavalry to her besieged fortress. The rest of her staff are composed of Miss Scott, the lower juniors teacher due for retirement, and Mrs. Pearson, in poor health, who, when fit to be present, takes charge of the infant class.

No-one offers me schemes of work and I do not ask to see any or even if they exist.

For the first time since my periods of school practice at college, I come in contact with a class of pupils who are lively, friendly, interested and able to think for themselves. It is a joy to me to read their original pieces of written work and to decorate the walls with the wonderful drawings of galleons which the boys produce in their spare time. I share their enjoyment of *Tom Sawyer* which I read to them daily in the last period of the afternoon as a reward for their quietness and hard work in other subjects. I do not acknowledge this as a form of bribery and I am quite horrified when I learn that Miss Scott, who shares an adjacent classroom to me, maintains her discipline by awarding sweets. It would appear that we both recognise the necessity for some system which, with only a glass partition between the classrooms, will afford us some degree of quiet in order to teach at all.

This might be quite the perfect school were it not for one family, namely the Craddocks. There are a number of Craddocks and in the school during my short stay there are three: Clarence, aged ten, Dorothy, aged nine and Ernest, aged eight. Both Clarence and Dorothy are in my class. I refrain from saying members of my class, as that phrase suggests that they share something in common with the rest and the Craddocks share nothing with the rest. With their own kin in school they squabble and fight and scratch and kick, but perhaps I do them an injustice as probably the home environment is such that they share everything from a bed to a bath.

Perhaps their individuality can only be manifested in the open rebellion we see in school.

To my knowledge the only luxury that the Craddocks share in abundance is ration books and with this bargaining power they rule our lives. To Miss Burton, barely subsisting on her meagre single ration book, the opportunity to purchase extra rations is beyond her powers of resistance.

It is an unwritten law that although the Craddocks are "difficult" they must never be punished but spoken to gently in order to be made to appreciate the errors of their ways. Thus, Ernest, whenever he feels thwarted, raises the lid of his desk, hurls the contents at the teacher and charges for the exit. Unfortunately for me the main exit cannot be reached except by way of my classroom so, while in the act of addressing my pupils, I am fairly frequently interrupted by Ernest's flight.

The first time this happens during my stay, the adjoining door is suddenly flung open and Ernest makes a headlong dash for freedom via the opposite door at the far side of my classroom. This is the signal for my boys to rise in a body and give chase. It all happens so quickly that any thought of action on my part is not even considered until the clatter of heavy boots tells me that my boys are hurling themselves down the stone steps which lead into the playground and the main gate. As the loyal warders explain to me later, it is essential that Ernest be caught before he reaches the street. On those occasions when he has succeeded in escaping, the headmistress has been forced to inform the police. It needs no further explanation. If only because she resents the curiosity of her neighbours, Mrs Craddock does not wish to have the police calling. Miss Burton prefers not to embarrass Mrs Craddock and possibly threaten the favours bestowed by that lady, so we are back in our vicious circle.

My boys continue to take the duties of the chase very seriously and, as they appear to settle down to their work quite peacefully on their triumphant return, I do not bear too heavy a grudge against the cause of the disturbance. I learn to listen for the warning signs as Ernest's books and pencils hit the blackboard and to stand clear of the escape route.

Clarence, in my class, is rather more my problem. He cannot or will not do any work and he frequently plays truant. On the days he does not put in an appearance we all get on so happily that it seems to me to be a pity that Miss Burton feels the need to pursue the cause of his absence, a course of action which results in his turning up in his usual place within the next day or two, just a distracting nuisance as far as the rest of us are concerned. Clarence refuses to conform to rules of attendance or punctuality or class instruction. The children accept that Clarence's regular attendance at the school guidance clinic marks him out as different, so it does not seem to them unfair that Clarence is not subject to the normal disciplinary rules.

At the clinic Clarence seems to spend most of his time making plaster models. I think the clinic is run by nuns as the figures which he brings in for my admiration tend to lean toward the religious. In a vague way I think he accepts my bogus admiration and is not unkindly disposed toward me. This is how I interpret the gift of a lump of plaster which he presents to me with a loquacious, "It's for you, Miss." The red clay is unpainted and it holds a vaguely human form. I decide not to risk my assumption that it is a Red Indian and merely say, "Thank you, Clarence, that's very kind of you but are you sure you don't want to keep it yourself?"

Clarence shakes his head, "No, Miss, you keep it. It's Jesus."

By contrast his sister, Dorothy, dislikes me and I dislike her. While Clarence has no wish to conform, retiring to his own private world and quietly refusing to acknowledge that anything exists outside it, Dorothy sets herself up as an anarchist intent on destroying anything which opposes her will. This takes the form of shouting and screaming at me and coolly marching up the aisles between the desks, deliberately hitting the other children with a ruler.

It seems to me that I try everything, ignoring her bad behaviour, putting her outside the classroom and even sending her to the headmistress, all without success. I do not try liking her, although I try to pretend to her that I like her. Miss Burton makes up for my deficiency in this respect. When she opens her door to find a dejected-looking but inwardly defiant Dorothy, it is her custom to express great surprise and immediately to create some little errand which Dorothy may carry out for her which will restore her to favour. Dorothy is absent for about half an hour and then returns, chaperoned by her protectress, who assures me that Dorothy has promised to be a good girl. It never works. Dorothy is never a good girl for me and it seems to me that beneath her assumed air of penitence she is barely concealing her grin of triumph.

Matters have to reach a climax and this they do one Friday afternoon during the last period of the day. The infant class and their teacher have been dismissed at three o'clock leaving the hall free, and for some reason Miss Scott has been allowed to leave early. Shortly after suggesting that I take the two junior classes together in the hall for a story, Miss Burton herself succumbs to one of her frequent attacks of migraine and leaves the building.

There are about seventy children sitting on the hall floor and all may yet be well if Dorothy were not one of the seventy.

I am but a few minutes into my story-telling when Dorothy decides this is far too peaceful and she can arouse some self-interest by fidgeting and interrupting each of my sentences. I try to ignore this but there is less tolerance from her neighbours who, as they voice their objections, are rewarded by a punch or a smack with the ruler. I try to wrest the offending weapon from her grasp and she struggles to hold on to it. I am not entirely blameless for the resulting "accidental" blow which strikes her on her bare arm. There is an uproar. She throws hysterics and the children cheer. It must seem to them that this is retribution for all the many times when she has got off scot-free.

Somehow the afternoon does reach its end and I go home exhausted and far from triumphant, knowing that I will have to face Dorothy again after the weekend. I retell the episode at home and my mother, as usual, comes up with a practical suggestion, "Be prepared for the next bout of hysteria. Have a jug of cold water within reach."

Fortified by this plan of campaign I return to school the following Monday. The children troop into the classroom but Dorothy is not among them. This is not unusual as frequently she runs messages for the headmistress before she joins the class. Presently Miss Burton appears to tell us all that Dorothy will not be returning to school for several weeks. During the weekend she has been knocked down by a car and is to undergo hospital treatment for an indefinite period. I do see Dorothy again. Some weeks later she returns, temporarily chastened by her recent experience but inwardly as sullen and resentful as ever. By this time I am not unduly worried by her re-appearance. I am looking forward to my release.

It is a pity that I should apply the word "release" to a situation which, by contrast to what I had endured beforehand, had seemed at first so pleasant but, over a period, I have come to realise that in this school there is little future. The actual cause of my departure is a row with the headmistress over a matter of honesty.

On the whole my relationship with Miss Burton is a friendly one. She allows me freedom of thought and, as far as she is able, of action. There are some small snags as, for example, when I suggest taking the class for some PE periods in the hall, a term we use euphemistically to describe the basement classroom where the furniture has been pushed back to allow some extra floor space. Almost always when I request the use of this room it is not convenient, often enough because Mrs Pearson is either coming in late or going off early and Miss Burton finds the hall facilities best for supervising the infants during her absence. To compensate for this, Miss Burton is willing to supervise my girls while I take the boys for football in the playground or to similarly take charge of the boys to allow the girls to play rounders. During the whole of my stay I have the class only three times for indoor PE.

On the first occasion I discover that this is an entirely new experience for my class. The boys much resent divesting themselves of jackets, pullovers and heavy boots. When I insist, there is every evidence of mutiny both in the form of mutterings and, in the case of two or three more boisterous types, actually flinging their belongings at one another.

After enduring about five or ten minutes of this bedlam I say that, as the behaviour is so appalling, we will return to the classroom and they will be deprived of an enjoyable activity. We collect our belongings and trail back upstairs where the muttering persists. I am thinking what a miserable failure of a lesson it has been and am about to call the class to order when I hear a muttered comment from the front desk. Peter, an easy-going boy by nature, sits supporting his head in his hands and in soliloquy utters the line, "When anybody's ready to listen to me, I've lost sixpence down in that madhouse."

As Miss Clarkson, our college lecturer in Educational Psychology, used to say, "If you want a true assessment of your lesson, look and listen for it to come from the children." How right she was!

My second indoor PE lesson is by comparison a model of decorum. The boys unwillingly part with outdoor boots and jackets and, as a reward, I allow them to use one end of the room for their ball activities while I supervise the girls' skipping. As we are thus engaged, a male visitor pokes his head in and quickly withdraws but I catch a brief glimpse of a clerical collar. This is later confirmed when Miss Burton tells me that earlier in the morning the local canon had paid her a visit and had gently enquired, "Who was the big girl who was turning the skipping rope for the younger girls?"

The boys and girls continue to enjoy the playground sessions of football or rounders. As far as the boys are concerned, one keeps on one's jacket and the noise created by their heavy footwear is acceptable out of doors so, when a PE inspector appears on the premises, it is unfortunate that she insists on observing an indoor lesson. Rising to the occasion the children behave reasonably well, but it is very evident that they lack regular training. The PE inspector comments on this and as politely as I can I explain the difficulties. She then leaves to report to the headmistress. At the end of the morning Miss Burton seeks me out to tell me of the bad report I have received from the PE inspector, who had further indicated that under the circumstances this was inevitable. She adds, "She seemed to have the impression that you had not been taking the regular periods set aside on the timetable for indoor PE, but I assured her that I was unaware of this lapse."

For a moment I think I have misunderstood what she is saying, then I say, "But you do know I haven't had the use of the hall and you also know why I haven't."

"So that is what you told her. I guessed as much. I left her in no doubt that you were trying to provide yourself with an excuse for your poor performance."

I hear myself protesting, "But you know that is not true."

That same day is the closing date for transfer applications for the forthcoming school year. With my probationary service about to end I am eligible to apply to a school of my choice where a vacancy is available. I have to make up my mind at once. I go home and pore over the list of schools requiring an assistant teacher. I see Greenfield Junior Girls. There is a familiar ring about that name, and then I remember.

During my probationary service at the last school we had, for one week, a supply teacher to replace an absentee member of staff. A pretty young girl, she brought a breath of fresh air into that prison house of one-track ideas. Like me she thought the conditions there were intolerable and she mentioned to me what a contrast these were to those she enjoyed in the school where she was fully employed. How I had envied her. Occasionally I still meet this attractive brunette on the second bus by which I travel to school. She alights from the bus one stop after I join it so our exchange has of necessity to be very brief. It consists of, from me, "Still at Green . . . ?" and from her, "Oh, yes. Wouldn't dream of leaving G . . ." Greenfield? Greenway ? Greenpark? All are listed with vacancies. Which is the one where she teaches? I take a chance on Greenfield and send in my application form.

One outing stands out in my brief time at T.D.Wavertree School. It is VE Day. As a celebration, Liverpool arranges for its cinemas to put on a show for all the schools to attend in the morning prior to the afternoon holiday. As a school we walk to the local Abbey Cinema to join a packed house of children from other neighbouring schools. There are cartoons and comedy films with a Western as a climax. Children laugh, clap, stamp, hoot and cheer. They drown the sound track but that does not detract from the overall enjoyment of the occasion.

I cannot think of VE Day without remembering that day and that school.

CHAPTER
FOUR

Greenfield School becomes my first love and as such remains the most vivid in my memory but on that September morning it is just a blind date.

Arriving on the premises early I am shown into the headmistress's room by the janitor. The building is not inspiring, a temporary wooden structure with a corrugated iron roof, set up after World War I and housing some two hundred infants and girls up to the age of eleven plus. Materially the boys fare better, their modern building being some five minutes walk away. As I wait in the little room, one by one the members of staff arrive. I am overjoyed to see Ruth, the teacher I have met on the bus; I have picked "the" school, but I am worried that it is coming up to nine o'clock and everybody seems quite content to stand and chat about the holidays. Presently the door is flung open and a mass of greenery appears. This is Miss Fletcher, my new headmistress, her hat askew and her arms laden with branches and plants of every description. To my astonished eyes she resembles Margaret Rutherford in one of her many successful film roles, or perhaps some jolly charlady. As she opens her generously large mouth and half panting, half laughing, the words come pouring out, my first impression remains unchallenged. She pumps everybody with questions, the answers to which she punctuates with sighs and gasps, exclamations of delight and a loud raucous laugh.

At long last (it must be 9.30 by this time), the staff depart to their classrooms and as a sequel to what now seems our far distant introduction she assures me that she hopes I will be very happy, but then she knows I will — such lovely children! and why not go along with her to meet my new class. From time to time as she speaks, in the meantime divesting herself of her outdoor clothes, there are knocks on the door and children coming and going and, she not one whit bothered that her hairpins are dropping out, for each and every child she has some personal greeting.

Finally we set off down the short corridor and in we go to the classroom where she is immediately greeted by shrieks of delight and forty children all trying to talk to her at once. "This," she tells me, "is my favourite class. Stand up, Sabrina. Ah! there's Sabrina. Where's Patsy? Oh! there you are, Patsy. Ah! yes, Laura, Naomi . . ." and so-on round the whole class. "I'll leave you to get to know them. You will enjoy yourself and do all sorts of wonderful things. Make the classroom look nice and bright. What are you planning to do? I expect you are brimming over with ideas."

Very primly I answer, "If you don't mind, I'll get the discipline first."

She smiles, "Ah!" as one might to a stray cat, then with a "See you later," she bounces out. Much later she is to remind me of my own remark and I am glad to say that by then I have sufficiently recovered my sense of humour to realise what a sorry figure I must have appeared.

There's a song in which comes the line "Eliminate the negative, accentuate the positive . . ." and I think that these words should be emblazoned in gold over the doorway of this school. Not that the words are at all necessary; one knows the moment that one steps into the building that here is a school with a difference, where everybody bubbles over with zeal and joy. No visitor to the school ever says, "What a dreadful building," despite the fact that in summer the tar on the roof melts so when it rains the floor is littered with pails to catch the water from the leaking roof. Instead these visitors enthuse about the beautiful flowers on every windowsill. No teacher ever says, "Jean is hopeless at Arithmetic." Instead she says, "Look at the lovely picture Jean painted." Nobody ever "fails". Even the lowest achiever in the class is "trying hard".

This is epitomised for me on one occasion when Miss Fletcher holds her weekly assembly. We have no hall but somehow, with a glass partition pushed back, the double classroom provides just enough space to pack everyone inside. Everything takes place in a very informal setting. Miss Fletcher refers to an occasion earlier that week when parents had been invited to see the children's work. In turn she comments on the contribution of each class and each member of staff, her remarks punctuated by the applause which she encourages. She pauses for breath and a hand goes up among the ranks. The child is invited to contribute which she does with, "And Mrs. Wilkinson tried hard, didn't she?" Mrs. Wilkinson is the motherly soul who comes in daily to supervise the cleanliness and escort of the girls who have their lunch in the boys' school across the road. There are a few smiles as Mrs Wilkinson receives her cheer. The system works like magic. From the youngest child to the oldest scrubber, a word of appreciation, an acknowledgement of effort and the world is transformed.

The magic works on me too. I doubt if I learn to teach in this school but I regain my desire to teach. I am allowed to make all the mistakes and to find out for myself which methods do not work. I hope that at some later date in their lives the children who passed through my hands managed to rectify the numerous wrong facts which I imparted, to glean some lasting interest from the mass of half-digested knowledge which I tried to impart and to escape not too badly maimed from the inconsistency of my methods. At this school I am not even aware when my classes are not learning at all in any real sense of the word. I do not go out of my way to create opportunities for pupil participation. I dominate the classroom with my ideas, my enthusiasms, relying on my own performance to somehow transmit these to the children and I honestly and foolishly think I am teaching. In the process my pupils must certainly suffer but I come to life and once again become a human being.

It all seems too wonderful to last and the day Miss Fletcher tells us that she has accepted a promotion to the headship of a senior girls' school I feel that my world is about to collapse. I have known her for a much shorter time than have the rest of the staff but whereas they are happy for her good fortune, I consider only the effect her departure will have on me. As a staff we are all quite sure that the new replacement will not be fit to buckle the shoes of the head we are losing and, with the vast experience of two former headmistresses behind me, I am certain that my sufferings are about to begin all over again. In this spirit we sit out the interval between heads. One event of some significance that happens during this period is a row we have with the head of the boys' department, a Mr Brookes.

It is the habit of our staff, four or five of us in our twenties, to join the older ladies, who teach the younger classes of the boys' department, in their staff-room for daily lunch, namely the school dinners we collect from the children's dining hall. For these dinners we pay the same price as that required from the children, the princely sum of two (shillings) and a penny per week and in return we take our turn on a daily rota of "dinner duty". Relationships between the teaching staff and the dining room attendants are a little strained partly, I suppose, because from time to time we find it necessary to complain about the food and because in their opinion we are too fussy. It is wartime and the food is pretty vile so, young and inexperienced as we are, we find it difficult to insist that the children eat the items which we ourselves refuse.

On the other hand we are able to observe that the dining room staff fare rather better. When the children have departed, they sit down to their free lunch accompanied, on more than one occasion, by a parcel of some tasty titbit to carry home. Unfortunately it is my duty day when the boiled ham, a luxury item, stretches to the plates of the staff and to all but a dozen children who receive only potatoes and beetroot for their main course. I accept Mrs Barrow's explanation until I realise that placed to one side under cover is a whole dish of sliced ham. Foolishly I confront Mrs Barrow with my discovery and after some argument it is decided that the matter will be referred to the headmaster. She manages to reach Mr Brookes with her version of the affair plus a complaint about my insinuations. Mr Brookes sends for me and wishes to know why I, a newcomer, have seen fit to offend Mrs Barrow who has worked alongside him for years. He brushes aside my explanation and demands my immediate apology to Mrs Barrow. This I refuse to give and as calmly as I can I say that I really do not understand why he should assume that I am lying about the incident and that Mrs Barrow is telling the truth. His reply is that he can assume what he pleases and that in the absence of our head I am under his jurisdiction and he expects me to acknowledge his right to judge correctly in this situation.

My colleagues take up cudgels on my behalf and demand a staff meeting with Mr Brookes. The meeting is a fiasco. Mr Brookes does all the talking and no-one else is given the opportunity to speak. Each time one of us attempts to speak she is silenced by his oft repeated, "Please do not interrupt me when I am speaking." As always under the stress of emotion which accompanies my sense of injustice I doubt whether I could have been coherent even if I had been given the chance.

Not so is the case with Beryl, the youngest and newest member of our staff who, having been silenced more than once by a quelling look and the words, "Excuse me. I am still speaking," holds her ground with an "Excuse me, Mr Brookes."

"I am speaking," snaps Mr Brookes.

Beryl remains on her feet and announces very firmly, "No, Mr Brookes, I am speaking."

He turns white with rage but Beryl gallantly persists in making her point.

She has breached his flood and in turn the various members of our staff add their support. It becomes clear that they have no intention of allowing a member of their staff to make any apology. If he doesn't see fit to take the word of a teacher on equal terms with that of a dining room attendant, then we have reached deadlock, and until such a time that he is prepared to do this he can keep his questionable dining room attendant, but he may also request from the head education office the services of a paid supervisor, as forthwith we refuse to undertake dinner duty in his building. Positions are now reversed, although we have reached stalemate rather than checkmate. Fortuitously Mr Brooke's retirement is imminent, Mrs Barrow disappears into oblivion and, after a period of tea and buns at the local teashop which plays havoc with our budget, the status quo is restored with one innovation.

It is from this date that the male members of staff join us for lunch. As a result of rumours which reach them concerning the "battle with Brookes", they have come to the conclusion that there is a bit of mettle in these youngsters who come over from the girls' department which it might be worth their while to challenge. Were it not that the male members of staff all enjoy marital status, we might better appreciate the attentions they are generous enough to bestow on us.

If Mr Wiseman and Miss Dickens, the two new heads of Greenfield, do not take up their appointments on the same date, it is within a very short interval of one another. He is tall, slim, good-humoured and in his early fifties, only in one or two mannerisms ever so slightly effeminate. She is a young, attractive well-groomed forty-year old in her first headship, with all the feminine wiles to aid a masculine efficiency. From the start it is obvious that they enjoy one another's company. They become friends and forge a great partnership which is to work to the mutual benefit of both staff and pupils.

Direct from her post as assistant head at Greensquare, where she practically ran the school while her superior presided over National Union of Teachers' affairs, she adversely criticises the low standard of achievement among our pupils and recognises the fact that with one exception she has in her staff a bunch of amateurs. Acknowledging that in her more mature vice-head she has a conscientious, hard-working teacher, she delegates to her most of the clerical work which can absorb so much of a principal's time and she throws herself into the job of putting Greenfield on the map as far as education is concerned.

She succeeds and in my opinion she succeeds because at the outset she does well the one job that a headteacher must do, that being the assessment and utilisation of the talents at her disposal. Also she is aware of her own strengths and abilities.

It always strikes me odd that in the teaching profession one secures one's promotion on one's ability to teach, yet the higher the promotion the less one is required to teach. I think that all headteachers should, if only occasionally, teach. This Miss Dickens does. She takes certain periods with each class in order to find out where the weaknesses lie. By this means she indirectly discovers which teachers have talents in certain directions and these she directs. Relieving the teacher who begins her music lessons by requesting a single pupil to "Sing doh, no, that's not doh," she suggests that for singing periods she might like to exchange her class with Miss Jefferson, leaving herself free to take Miss Jefferson's class for poetry or music and movement. Thus, although remaining a primary school where, in the main, teachers are non-specialist, she gives each of her staff the chance to promote interest and zeal with more than one class in a subject of her own choice, where it is likely she will experience some degree of success.

One teacher becomes the music specialist for several classes and soon we have a school choir, another takes country dancing and soon the headmaster is asking if she can be loaned to his boys to introduce them to country dancing. She develops this to such a degree that she has the boys tackling Cossack dances and

Scottish sword dances, while another teacher forms a speech choir to enable her pupils to better enjoy their poetry lessons.

I am allowed to find my own way into mime and movement to recorded music. I start with a very simple class interpretation of *The Teddy Bears' Picnic* and because I had seen the ballet of *Peter and the Wolf* danced on the professional stage my class and I work out a simplified version which we perform on Parents' Day.

Miss Dickens does not impose her own ideas but she encourages and praises and we become her willing slaves. She throws open the school to inspection by parents, local inspectors and H.M.I.s. She milks them of their ideas and these she incorporates. It is flattery in its most subtle form and she develops it into a fine art. She uses the same tactics with Mr Wiseman and before long we are sharing their peripatetic pianist and their hall in return for our including the boys in some of the drama classes for which I am responsible.

Before long we are all cooperating in a joint effort. On the surface our first use of combined talents and facilities takes the form of a Christmas show. I use the poem of *The Raggle Taggle Gypsies* for the continuity story line, with a minstrel miming to the refrain sung by the choir. The minstrel is performing for the mediaeval court so we are able to include mummers with the hobby horse acting out the story of St George and the Dragon. We have a jousting scene and tumblers to feature the boys. The court ladies perform their dances to the music of *Greensleeves* and the final scene celebrates Christmas with some of the lesser-known old carols such as *Wassail* and *Rumpty Tum Tum*.

Using the interest which the children have in the "show", we use our history lessons to teach about the life of the Knight, the Squire, the Page and other characters which symbolise the Middle Ages, so the whole becomes a teaching project rather than just a performance. On the three nights we give the performance, we have over a hundred children in costume plus a choir and Miss Dickens prevails upon her own dramatic society to provide the lighting and make-up.

The next year we carry out a geography project. Our choice of country is somewhat determined by our research, which provides us with the Russian legend of Baba Yaga, the songs and dances of Hungary, Spain and Norway and the New Year festivals of China. The story which links the scenes is that of five puppets who come to life and go out to seek the gift their country can bestow, so we call it *Quest for Happiness*.

We make Ireland the centre of our third project, creating a story line to incorporate several Irish legends, folk songs and dances. We start with an idea and develop a script as we go along. As in our other productions, it is only about a dozen children whom we can rely on to learn and deliver the spoken lines, and we use them for the continuity of the story between the scenes of dance and mime.

In 1951, the year we celebrate the Festival of Britain, London has its Festival Hall and its Battersea playground, but Greenfield produces a marathon effort which starts with the monk Caedmon and concludes with a human ship to illustrate the poetry of Masefield. It includes excerpts from Chaucer's *Canterbury Pilgrims*, Shakespeare's *Henry the Fifth*, Milton's masque of *Comus*, Tennyson's *Lady of Shalott* and others selected to indicate the contribution these writers made to our national heritage. We call it *Lode Star*.

Different groups of children under different teachers work to develop parts of each scene. I work with the groups responsible for carrying the story line and much of the free movement and mime and, towards the end, with the whole cast. I think this is the kind of situation in which much is caught rather than taught. Earlier in this chapter, I admitted that my classroom procedure was teacher-orientated and teacher-dominated, leaving little scope for pupil participation and real learning. I am now discovering that with children involved in any form of production, the learning situation is established. It is present by its very nature and I do not have to contrive it. How do I know this? I know it happens because we are all working towards one goal and all determined to give of our best. It is not a selfish goal as each child realises that the part he plays is dependent on another playing his part. If he forgets his lines or his position on the stage it affects someone else. He may even find himself working overtime to cover up for someone else making a mistake.

It is the kind of learning which will stand him in good stead for life long after the history or the geography facts have been forgotten. He learns the value of cooperation, of working in unison and of experiencing the satisfaction of a job well done. He learns to think through his imagination, to become, if but for a short while, someone other than himself so he is no longer dependent on a teacher telling him how to portray the character he has assumed. He learns to be critical, he learns to appreciate and he learns that the child who came bottom of the class in the arithmetic test can become a star under a spotlight. He learns the valuable lesson that each human being has worth. The children discover the best kind of discipline which is self-discipline. If someone is noisy off stage awaiting his turn to perform, it could drown out his music cue and knowing this he will behave when he is off stage.

There are many nights when members of staff stay on at school after four o'clock to make costumes and scenery. We bring sandwiches or send out for fish and chips. There are other nights when the children return after tea for the rehearsals we cannot fit into the school day. It is often after ten o'clock when I get home and my mother inquires why I don't have a bed at school.

It might be supposed that with so much of my time happily engaged in school activities there would not be the opportunity for much of a life outside school, yet the contrary is true. Our headmistress organises parties, inviting her friends from the drama group she supports to partner her young staff in Scottish country dance evenings, when we use the school hall and she provides the buffet.

For some years now I have been a member of a drama group and although there is still a dearth of

58

young men, as many are not yet released from the armed forces, we find plays with a predominately female cast and perform *Ladies in Retirement, Night Must Fall* and *The Corn is Green* during these immediate post-war years. I enjoy ballroom dancing and regular cinema outings with a variety of boyfriends.

One friend from schooldays works as a chartered secretary in a firm which employs several young men. With four of them and another three girl friends of mine we have regular Saturday outings. We end up in my home where, with tea and sandwiches, we monopolise the sitting room, imitating the vocal renderings of The Inkspots and playing Twenty Questions. One of the couples decides to become engaged and, feeling threatened by the awesomeness of this, the group disintegrates although some of us meet up again from time to time.

Summer weekends find me in the Wirral countryside, at Southport or rowing on the Dee at Chester. Since finishing training college I've used some of every summer holiday to go youth-hostelling. Once my loan is paid back over my first five years of teaching, I can even afford to stay at guest houses. In this way I get to know North Wales, the Cotswolds and the Thames Valley. I regularly visit friends in London where, because they are both working, I am on my own for most of the day. I attend lunchtime concerts at the National Gallery, open-air performances of Shakespeare in the London parks and, for the price of a sixpenny stool in a morning queue, I can secure my cheap seat in the gods of most of the London theatres. I see Celia

Johnson in Eliot's *Cocktail Party*, a young John Gielgud in Christopher Fry's *The Lady's not for Burning* and Moira Shearer in *The Sleeping Beauty* at Covent Garden. Each year I manage an overnight stay at Stratford in order to fit in both matinee and evening performances, the most memorable being *Much Ado About Nothing*, *The Tempest* and *King Lear*. If my memory is correct, I think Tyrone Guthrie was the man responsible for the productions during this period.

Penguin paperbacks are available, often at one or two shillings. I get hooked on crosswords, the *Poetry Quarterly Review* and the *Argos* short story magazine, but I also read anything I can get my hands on by Graham Greene, H. E Bates and Nevil Shute.

There's little time left for anything but a passing interest in the men in my life but I manage to fall hopelessly in love with three of them. The first of these is nine years my senior and I admire him from that distance, wishing that I was as mature as the lady to whom he becomes engaged, unaware of my breaking heart. He remains a lifetime friend. The second is a warrant officer in the R.A.F. I am bowled over by his uniform, his beguiling smile and his Scottish accent. I see him regularly while he is stationed near Liverpool but only once after he is demobbed and returns to civvy street in Glasgow. The third I meet for the odd week or two weeks on three or four holidays spread over a period of five years and, yes, I marry him and not without some sadness I leave Greenfield.

While I am still at Greenfield in the early 1950s, one inspector, sitting in on a hall lesson in which the children are interpreting the music in the form of movement and mistaking me for an enthusiast, suggests that I enrol for a one-week summer course to be carried out in Dartington Hall in Devon.

As it turns out, this course, which is supposed to be a holiday course, is dated for the week after northern schools have already reassembled for the autumn term, so there is some question as to whether or not I will be allowed to participate. After much negotiating I am not only permitted to attend but I am also paid my full salary for what is virtually an extra week's holiday and a very entertaining experience.

I take advantage of the postscript attached to the invitation to Dartington Hall and for an additional small fee accept the offer of a weekend on the premises prior to the course beginning on the Monday. When I arrive I find that the company consists of hangovers from the previous week's drama course plus new arrivals like myself who have enrolled for the modern dance. I drift into the company of the drama folk and thoroughly enjoy the weekend.

When they depart on the Sunday evening I am aware that the atmosphere has somewhat changed. Instead of noisy, garrulous groups all competing for an audience, the place now acquires the air of a religious retreat. There is the odd "theologian" talking in what is to me incomprehensible language, surrounded by a little clique of "disciples" gathered at his feet, hanging on his every word.

I retire to my bedroom to find that my two room-mates have done likewise. I refer to the company we have left downstairs and am greeted by gales of laughter. "Just wait until Monday," I am told, "You've seen nothing yet."

I say that I take it they have attended this course before and I ask if it tends to be the same people who attend each year. "Indeed, yes," they assure me, "It's a matter of religious observance with most of them. Not like us. We come for the laughs."

Monday morning dawns and not without some trepidation I join my two room-mates in the gymnasium, clad as are all the other females in cuttysarks. The one or two males are dressed in cricket gear, which garb has some later significance. We prance about as directed. We are strong or light, slow or quick, direct or flexible with thrusts and flicks and punches, the computations of which are innumerable. We become trees, waves, flowers and bubbles and believe me, even with imagination, in most cases the result is ludicrous. We are assured throughout that it is the "feeling" which counts. We must "feel" the movement.

Later in the day we attend the first of the lectures and I am introduced to the high priest of the movement. Through a study of work done in factories Professor Laban has developed the idea that movement can evoke mood, thought and speech. Perhaps it is my misinterpretation, but while I vaguely accept the idea that if I relax physically I will relax mentally, I cannot quite clear the reverse hurdle that if I have belligerent feelings I will feel less belligerent when I have finished doing my thrusting and punching. What interests me much more than the content of the lecture is the attitude of the students. No-one questions the truth of the gospel and when, in group discussion later, I dare to suggest that some of the theories at the basis of the teaching are more than a little open to doubt, it is made quite clear to me that I am the only admitted heretic in the company.

During the week we continue to attend the lectures but the activities are the mainstay of the course. As well as the general movement classes we are on several occasions taken by Madame X who, through encouraging freedom of movement, is I think trying hard to influence our souls. She tells us that mankind is divided into three main groups, the thinkers, the feelers and the workers, and we may choose the group to which we wish to become aligned. After some brief demonstration of how these types behave, it seems to me that as a worker I am being called upon to grovel round the floor and use up far too much energy, while as a feeler I am being asked to look quite ridiculous, a cross between an overweight fairy and an astronaut struggling to get out of his space suit. I elect to join the thinkers as, standing on two feet, they seem to be the only group who are going to manage to hang on to their shreds of human dignity. Having been dispatched to three corners of the room, we have now to advance on our opposing groups and react. I haven't a clue what to do but at the front of the thinking group I spring to life in answer to the yell from Madame X. Our group, from standing stiffly to attention like a bunch of robots, move suddenly forward in a diagonal direction, arms raised, true Nazi-style, eyes forward, stiff-limbed, aloof from any involvement with the rest. From their respective corners both workers and feelers surge forward round about the level of our knees to entangle with one another in the central floor space. As we, the thinkers, are still standing unbloodied, unbowed and uncontaminated by the rest of "humanity", I congratulate myself that the thinkers emerged as the winners in this mêlée.

"Words come through movement" is another section of the gospel in which we are to be thoroughly drilled by a yet more ancient madame. In these classes it is regularly stressed that relaxation and correct breath control lie at the basis of good speech and while I gladly agree, my dignity balks at kneeling on all fours and, like a dog, panting and letting my tongue hang out. As a further progression each group receives a copy of the same poem to be interpreted in speech and movement. We are allowed time to develop this before being called upon to perform, each in turn. In our group we have rehearsed our roles of rocks, clouds and lashing spray but in this group we have a gentleman and it is he that provides us with our pièce de resistance. As our final line is delivered, he rises from his squatting position behind the "rocks", beautifully timed to match the eloquence of "And from the rocks rose one white seagull", and this white-haired gentleman of some sixty summers totters ungracefully to his feet clad in his white cricket trousers and sweater.

It would be unfair to suggest that I receive no benefit from the course. Apart from the immediate benefit of enjoying the humour of it all, some of the principles do influence my pupil classes. Nevertheless, by rejecting the mystique, I doubt if I can ever be accepted as a true disciple of Laban. Some ten years later I glance at a PE syllabus for Scottish schools and I am amazed that the dance section contains indisputable evidence that the leaven is working its way through the lump and the teaching once reserved for a sacred few has become available to the masses.

While I had been down in Devon, Greenfield had been ravaged by a fire and I return to chaos. Of the seven classrooms only four remain, so two of our classes are housed in the boys' department and it falls to my lot to take lessons with the remaining refugees in the church hall opposite the school. I say "to take lessons" rather than to teach because "teaching" becomes an impossibility.

When we arrive each morning our first task is to set up half a dozen benches and trestle tables. When my eight-year olds are seated, their chins rest on the tables while their legs dangle inches above floor level. If they need to write they kneel on the floor and rest their work on the bench. I cannot see all of them unless I peer below the tables and, except for the children at the front, most of them are only seeing my legs and feet. For the morning and afternoon intervals we cross the road for the sake of making use of the playground and the toilets. At the end of six months a third classroom becomes available in the boys' department so we are not sorry to leave the church hall.

The department is eventually to be reunited but this does not happen until after I have left. I make one visit to the new school, certainly a beautiful building, spacious and well-lit, with a modern assembly hall complete with a stage. Taking tea in the staff-room, it seems to me that the atmosphere of the bad old days can never be recaptured. Then, when we had taken tea without a staff-room, we had done so balancing on four washbasins in the pupil washroom, and how true it was that the absence of luxury stimulated the mind, for it was in this close contact that we had exchanged all our best ideas.

Since I married I have enjoyed several luxury holidays in hotels, but in none of them did I find such lively minds as those I encountered amid the bare furnishings of youth hostels. In my day youth was persistently penniless and one of the few enjoyments we could afford was unlimited conversation. In the new Greenfield School it seems to me that one has to worry far too much about wearing the correct footwear in order to preserve the polished floors. The homesickness which I felt for earlier times is cured. The Greenfield school I had known no longer exists.

Of that period in my teaching career two or three outstanding memories remain and they are of individual children. There was Stuart who danced as Peter in *Peter and the Wolf*, a mischievous eight-year old who inspired the rest of the cast with his imagination and agility. There was Todd who won my heart for his performance of the title role in a scene from *Henry the Fifth*. There was Brenda, a child who found it difficult to remember anything from one lesson to the next in a classroom, who waylaid me one morning in a great state of excitement because the previous evening she had recognised the music from *Scheherezade* played on the radio as the music we used to represent a storm in which she danced as the figurehead in the prow of the ship.

Best of all I remember Sheila Green. Sheila was one of the puppets in *Quest for Happiness* but the incident I recall took place in a classroom situation. Each Monday morning we set aside the first fifteen minutes for a few children to take it in turn to stand facing the class to retell some event which had taken place at home during the weekend. Sheila was the best storyteller. She had a younger sister, Pearl, and a younger brother, Paul, in lower classes of the school and there were many older Greens at home, some of whom were earning a living. We all enjoyed the stories Sheila told about her family, how the older members sat at the table to eat and only when they were finished was there room for Sheila and other younger children to have their meal. There must have been about twelve in the family and a parrot who whenever the mother entered the room called out, "What a smasher!"

It was a day following a national holiday for the wedding of Princess Elizabeth and Prince Philip. Back at school the children wanted to talk about the photographs of the wedding dress and the ceremony which adorned the morning newspapers. One or two children talked to the rest about how they spent the holiday. Few if any Liverpool children could have joined the London crowds. It was Sheila's turn to talk to the class. Eyes opened wide in surprise and admiration as Sheila told us how she and her family went to London and were guests at the wedding. She described in detail the crowds in the streets, the cheering, the bands and the clatter of the horses' hoofs in the procession, all of which were left behind when they went to the palace "for tea".

I knew it was all a creation of her vivid imagination but it would have been cruel of me to have so accused her. I said, "Thank you, Sheila, you told that story very well," but privately I asked her if the family had travelled by train. Without hesitation she assured me that they had gone in her brothers' lorry and stood on it to view the proceedings before going to the palace. Later I met Pearl on the corridor. "What did you do on your holiday?" I asked.

"We played tiddly-winks on the table," she said, "But Sheila fell asleep on the sofa, listening to the radio."

CHAPTER
FIVE

The wet October holiday that I become engaged to a Glaswegian necessitates the bold action on my part of applying for a teaching post in Glasgow. Having from various sources gained the impression that Scottish education is somewhat superior to any elsewhere in the British Isles, and knowing that my certificate entitles me only to practise teaching south of the border, it is with some trepidation that, at the reception desk in the Glasgow Education Office, I ask meekly, "Do you have any vacancies?" It does not help to overcome my sense of inferiority when the clerk asks, "For school cleaners?" Admittedly my new primrose raincoat is a little the worse for wear for a week of rain and city soot but, struggling to maintain a little dignity, I reply, "No. For teachers." I am handed the application forms and immediately on my return to Liverpool I post off the three-month required notice and throw my financial future into the lap of Saint Andrew or more correctly Saint Mungo.

Most of my correspondence is with Edinburgh and as time wears on and I fill in form after form, it seems to me that of all the possible qualifications for the post, mine are the most meagre. To give but one example:

Please indicate qualifications as follows;

a) Honours Graduate, b) Ordinary Graduate, c) Four year Training College course, d) Three year Training College course, e) Any other training you think may be considered acceptable.

In all questions of this nature I am proving myself the least eligible applicant in that, during the war, one was only trained for two years in English colleges. Even in the question concerning religious denomination I feel that by writing Anglican I am sealing my own death warrant.

I do not bargain for the acute shortage of teachers in Glasgow and my Christmas Eve interview with the staffing official is quite a gay, abandoned affair. All he apparently wishes to ascertain is that I have a degree of physical fitness which will get me to the nearest bus stop and a standard of mental alertness to enable me to alight at the correct school. A body to stand in front of a class is obviously all that is needed.

"Of course," he says, "You realise you will have to teach uncertificated here. You won't get full pay. You can start negotiating to see if the authorities will accept your nine years' teaching experience in lieu of training." I nod my acceptance and he goes on, "You'll be carrying on after you are married? Well, that's all. You will receive your official appointment by post. You've got the job."

I dance down Sauchiehall Street despite the Christmas Eve crowds. This is my passport to paradise.

I have a teaching job. I can afford to pay my digs in Glasgow, which means that, for the first time since we became engaged, my fiancé and I can enjoy a relationship other than that allowed by correspondence. More materially we can start looking for a house, which acquisition we have determined will set our wedding date.

Christmas and New Year come and go and, as the new term does not begin until mid-February, so in fact do my meagre savings. Two months' board to pay with no salary, but I must admit that it never enters my head to try to get work serving in a shop or in an office during this interval when there is so much else to do. We decide on a house almost immediately, the only new housing being built on the south side of Glasgow at this time. From then on I am kept busy losing my way round Glasgow, visiting warehouses and stores, selecting linoleum, carpets, curtains and furniture. There is never a moment to spare and it is difficult indeed to fit in the time to put in my first appearance at David McLeod Primary school.

Of this episode in my career the less said the better. I tolerate it. I cannot say that it affects my happiness because at this time nothing outside of my love life is of any consequence. I have a kindly, understanding landlady, I am well-fed, I have a lovely room and my life is completely full without school. School is just a necessary chore and in a sense I enjoy disliking it. Inwardly I am appalled by what passes under the guise of education in this barren wilderness, but I keep my criticism to myself and, worse still, I keep my conscience quiet by telling myself that, as one of the lesser brethren, it is in no way my responsibility to try to change the status quo.

My impression of the staff-room is that it is nauseating. Staff members are already deep in a bridge game when the nine o'clock bell sounds and the game is continued at lunch time and at intervals throughout the day. Everybody appears to be so thoroughly au fait with everything to the exclusion of how to make school a happy environment for the pupils. In the classrooms and on the stairs and corridors all the staff seem to yell at the children, and in the staff-room there is constant moaning about the hooligan behaviour. As one teacher so aptly sums up the attitude preponderant throughout the school, "School would be quite tolerable without the kids. Have we got time for another rubber before the bell?"

As with most unpleasant things I remember little of this short episode in my school career. One or two incidents remain vivid. One such incident is the time when I first have to use the strap. At first sight, the strap reclining in the drawer of the teacher's desk resembles some mediaeval weapon. I do not know which end to grasp and there and then I make up my mind that I will never use it. Those who argue in its defence will see it only as the equivalent of the cane used in English schools, but in Corporation primary schools only the principal has access to it. Only in extreme cases does a teacher admit defeat and refer breaches of discipline to the head of the department. I

72

cannot think of a single instance when it is used for failure in academic attainment.

Without the strap I manage well enough in my classroom. I don't make too many demands on my class and I spend most of my time trying to find out what, according to the subject theme bible, they are supposed to have already learned. This is a tricky business because for several months my pupils have been through the hands of a series of teachers who for one reason or another have abandoned them. May I hasten to add that, in this respect, I am no better than my predecessors and the teacher who is to follow me will find her task even more difficult.

The biggest snag to our peace is that classrooms are divided by a very thin glass partition so all sounds penetrate from one room to the next. My nearest neighbour has to suffer the chanting of my class and of me. I am rather diffident about broadcasting but compared with me she is a pro. Her normal speaking voice would match creditably with the volume of any staunch football fan so that, when she wishes to convey her displeasure, it practically shatters the glass. Added to this she wields the strap with great flourish. It is her regular procedure to line up the pupils who have failed to obtain full marks in the daily spelling test and these she belts. If she enters a noisy classroom, the punishment is meted out in turn to each member of the class so it consumes a great deal of her time.

In our class we are all so busy listening to the harangue going on next door that seldom do we raise our voices above a whisper lest we miss something. My pupils are friendly and in their company I cheerfully acquire most of the Glasgow slang, together with the worst Glaswegian accent, and this I tend to unwittingly trot out while being entertained by my fiancé's refined relatives. I am trying so hard to eliminate the contempt for the English which I figure must have existed since the Battle of Bannockburn. I have only to mark the work which the children have written at my dictation to realise that we speak a different language and that, like the biblical Ruth, I am knee deep in alien corn.

Alas, the day comes when I am to bite the chaff. A student has taken over the class next door. Knowing that she is not allowed to use the strap, the rebels in her class deliberately behave badly and the silence of the afternoon is wrecked by her frantic attempts to maintain discipline. Presently one of her pupils is sent to report to me, "Please, Miss, the teacher says you've to belt me." I don't know who is more staggered, my class or myself as I fumble for the belt and flick it over the miscreant's palm. I miss. He remains standing with his hand outstretched anticipating some second attempt on my part so, to add to my confusion, I am forced to dismiss him hurriedly. There is no way I am going to risk missing the target for a second time.

For a very brief period it might seem to outward appearances that I never had it so easy. I rarely see the headmaster but his second in command pops in regularly to check on pupil attendance and I receive frequent little notes from him when weekly totals justify a reward. This reward takes the form of the class being allowed to dismiss an hour early on Friday afternoons,

74

a happy bonus for a newly married teacher who then has time to do her weekly shopping on the way home. There are similar perks. As most of my needlework class have already finished the piece of work in hand and there being no further supply of material for them to embark on anything new, they willingly sew tapes on all my personal dish-towels and dusters, thus giving my visitors the mistaken impression that I am a systematic housewife.

One inspector crosses my threshold during the months I am in that school and he asks me to take a reading lesson. I give the most appalling class reading lesson, one which would most certainly have been severely criticised by my college tutor. The children take it in turn to read round the class, a very dated procedure. I ask the occasional unprepared question on content or draw attention to some particular word. I wait to be taken to task but at the close of the lesson the inspector mumbles some phrases about satisfactory procedure and class management. I am left with the assurance that I have not failed although everything I have ever learned denies this.

It must be May before I become quite certain that I am pregnant and with delight I realise that my days of this parasitic existence are numbered. I tread the corridors with a lighter step and can smile tolerantly at the grumbling of my colleagues, yet I still acquiesce by my silence. In the privacy of my classroom I resist the temptation to display a bit of courage by scrapping some of the outdated text books. I am to stay here for just a few more weeks and to be a renegade is just too much effort and, in any case, I am having great difficulty not nodding off in some of the afternoon sessions. I have decided on the limited experience of two or three short months in one Glasgow school that the whole system of Scottish education is a sham. To me with my English prejudice it seems years behind English education and I cannot tolerate the smugness with which it is conducted.

Were it not that a teacher of any kind is as valuable as gold in Glasgow at this time, I do not imagine I would have even been considered for this appointment but if I have any doubts on this matter they are laid to rest by a telephone conversation I have with some representative at the Education Office. On my making it clear that my service will be terminating more quickly than I had planned, I am told "You may teach until a date three months ahead of the anticipated date of the birth. Then you must resign but you will continue to draw salary until the actual birth date. You are permitted to resume duties when the child is three months old."

I hasten to assure this speaker that in my case the ruling must be somewhat different as I am an unqualified teacher and I am certain that I will not, definitely not, be returning to teaching. My remark is dismissed as irrelevant and in the months which follow, as each pay slip is delivered, I manage to conquer my inhibitions which make me feel like a refugee poaching on Scottish charity.

No amount of subtle planning could have enabled me to receive such a maximum benefit from such a minimal effort. I teach until we break up at the end of June. I collect salary throughout the long summer holiday. I work one week of August and then idle away the last three months anticipating motherhood, all the while collecting salary until our daughter is born on December 7th, exactly nine months from the day we were married. At some point during that interim period I receive a letter which ironically informs me that my years of "experience" have paid off. I am now recognised as a fully certificated member of the Scottish teaching profession, the additional difference in salary to be backdated from the week I had taken up the appointment. As I waddle round in the advanced stages of pregnancy, it is a great boost to my morale to have it in writing that, in this alien land, I, a foreign immigrant, am classified as a fully qualified educator.

CHAPTER
SIX

The fifth school, though having only one teacher and one pupil for part of the time and later one teacher and two pupils, is the smallest but the most difficult of all. There are no intervals and no friendly or even unfriendly staff to chat with and, as every parent discovers, one pupil can be as demanding as fifty.

I stay there for the best part of six years and am still working in this school when, as my pupils reach their teenage years, I look back and realise that for a long time they have been the teachers and I have been the pupil.

Like every parent, I have long since told every story I know and have been presented with all the questions, the answers to which I do not know. I discover that discipline is an art which ceases to function at the moment in every mother's day when the phone is ringing, the bread van is at the door and the soup is boiling over. I am learning that black is no longer black and white is no longer white and that I myself am the most inefficient, disorganised and inconsistent parent. As never before I believe in the doctrine of original sin; how else to explain how essentially selfish and egotistical is every small child? As never before I believe in a power for good beyond anything man can do; how else to explain that despite all our failure our children grow up to be normal human beings. All this is by the way, of course, and learning to become a parent is not part of this story. The reason I mention it is because for me it provides some insight into the mind of the child which sends me back into teaching with a light heart.

The fifth school proper is the local primary school which my six-year old daughter attends and the introduction comes when, in one particularly difficult staffing period, the headmaster has nobody to stand in front of one of his classes. This then is my first function at the school in which I am to teach for the next thirteen years.

When approached by my daughter's teacher to help out for a week, I point out that I have no alternative but to bring my three-year old with me. This I do and he, being a placid little chap, plays each morning with his Dinky cars in one corner of the classroom and just as placidly each afternoon he falls asleep on the classroom floor. I feel so guilty that, halfway through the week, I beg to be released but bend to the plea of the headmaster that I complete the week as it will be impossible for him to get a replacement in midweek. I discover later that it is the finance department in Bath Street who find their sums too difficult if they have to work out the pay for fractions of a week.

I enjoy myself with the class and my happiness knows no bounds when some time later I receive the cheque for my week's service. It is a wonderful cheque, a figure of twenty pounds for just five days, at a time when my housekeeping budget is limited to the seven pounds a week which my husband sets aside from his wage. I put it in the post office savings bank and, for what seems an age, I feel I have a source of private income.

A year later the same headmaster asks me to consider returning for a whole term's teaching. One of his teachers has retired and if he cannot get a replacement he will need to split the class among his already overburdened staff. My husband and I decide that our son is of an age to possibly benefit from nursery school so, very much for what we regard as a trial period, I go back to teaching.

At the end of the term I receive a letter of thanks for my service and when the school holidays are over I receive a second letter requesting my services at the school for the following year. This procedure is repeated over the next ten years. I am employed as a temporary, full-time teacher receiving a salary calculated on a higher daily scale to compensate for my non-entitlement to holiday pay. I am happy with this arrangement, aware that if the need arises for me to be at home because of the illness of one of my children I will not feel conscience-smitten about unpaid absence.

It is probably true to say that without intending it, and with the exception of Greenfield, in all the other schools so far I have lived out a lie. With the children I have pretended to a dignity I did not possess. With members of staff or parents who were frequently a generation older than me I pretended to a wisdom I had never gained. I saw everything as right or wrong. I was youthful and rebellious and had little toleration for anything that was not the fruit of modern thinking. As I worked by the tried and trusted methods that were thrust upon me, I despised myself for so conforming. It is only with hindsight that I see I lacked the courage to introduce my own ideas. I convinced myself that I was teaching and for most of the time I had not even started to learn to teach. This is what this book is about. It is full of my intolerance, my criticism of others and my very immature judgements which at the time I felt justified in sustaining. One might say that training college gave me the highway code, the letter of the law, the principles of teaching to be used and adapted in the light of experience. When I meet with the inevitable bumps and scrapes I blame the other drivers. I can see clearly how they are misusing the road but I fail to see that I am ever at fault.

Perhaps the main reason I enjoy teaching at Limewood School is because I am content to be myself. When, as a Mum, one works in a local school it is impossible to keep up any pretence. Some of the girls I teach have, as toddlers, pushed their toy prams in my garden, have had cross words with my precocious daughter in her bullying infancy. Some of the boys in my class have dropped jellies on my dining room carpet and have trodden mud up my stairs. All at times see me at the bread van with my hair in curlers, collecting the doorstep milk in my dressing gown, cleaning the windows or scrubbing the steps in my working trousers. I am rushing to hang out last-minute washing as they set off for school and I am putting the shopping list into the grocer as the school bell is about to ring. The children accept me as a teacher in school but outside school I am just another Mum.

Yet another of Miss Clarkson's maxims comes to mind: "With every pupil one must work from the known to the unknown." Living locally gives me a head start in this direction. I can use any number of things to spark off or recall the children's interest. I mention Miss Glen's and every child knows I am talking about the little shop halfway down the hill which sells everything. For many of them it was the first place to which they were allowed to venture solo before they reached school age, because the excursion did not involve crossing any major road.

My class knows all about my automatic cooker because, in Arithmetic lessons, I refer to it and the calculations which need to be made in order to set the timer. Similarly the children are familiar with my kitchen that, with three glass walls and a perspex roof, can readily provide me with the examples of temperature change and condensation.

With the children themselves, I see them no longer as angels or fiends. The little mite who never stops chatting to her neighbour is an only child and, with no siblings at home for her to talk to, she seizes every chance to share company at school. The child who wants to be chosen for every job, who is willing to arrive early and stay late, is the child whose mother is out at a job from 8.30a.m. to 5.30p.m. The child who produces no homework for a week is being looked after by a neighbour while his mother is in hospital and he is probably crying himself to sleep every night.

With the parents it is no longer an effort for me to talk on the same wavelength. I can appreciate their very real difficulties and I sometimes wish that I could not quite so clearly recognise those parents who are only pretending to care.

I thoroughly enjoy the company of my colleagues. Like me some of them are married with families. My husband says he would not have the headmaster's task for a princely salary. I ring up the headmaster one morning because I cannot leave the house. A huge kitchen window has been blown out by the overnight gales and I have to be on the premises until the glazier can be persuaded to risk life and limb in replacing the glass in the continuing high winds. Another married colleague is late because the central heating engineer promised to arrive in her lunch hour. It is now two o'clock and he still hasn't arrived. Always there are the occasions when someone has to take their own child to the hospital or even stay off school to nurse him through measles or chickenpox.

At Limewood I am essentially a class teacher with no opportunity to be part of a larger joint effort, as I had at Greenfield, but my classes come to expect that at some time during the year they will in one way or other be contributing toward a performance. This can often take the form of a nativity play which we produce in a stageless hall for the rest of the school, very simple, with the audience joining in the carols. One year I have an outstanding class so we rehearse extracts from *Toad of Toad Hall*. The scenes from the wild wood are mimed to music and most of the class take part, but the four children who take on the main characters find their own time to learn and rehearse their lines. In handwork we make our own animal masks, parents help me with simple costumes, and we do invite them to join the audience when we perform it for the school. Another year I combine classes with a teacher of the class adjoining mine who is young enough to be my daughter. She takes on all the staging, props and costumes, and is responsible for the songs which form the continuity while I use children from both classes to mime to recorded music and finally perform *The Sleeping Beauty*. We surprise ourselves with the positive outcome which is achieved, especially among the more reticent children.

The *Sleeping Beauty* songs are introduced through a radio series for schools called *Time and Tune*. This is but one of many radio or television school programmes which inspire the correlation of several subjects over a period of weeks. The teacher's handbook accompanying each series contains many suggestions on how this might be achieved, through linking art, handwork, creative writing and other activities.

It is during these years at Limewood that I discover the C. S. Lewis books in the series that begins with *The Lion, the Witch and the Wardrobe*. I make time in a busy week to read these books aloud to my class.

The first year of my service at Limewood coincides with the Russian Yuri Gagarin travelling into space. Inspired by the common enthusiasm for this event, we use our history and art lessons to make a pictorial history of our own time to mount on the classroom walls. We attempt to illustrate a chapter of history that their own children will find in their history books a quarter of a century on. My headmaster expresses his approval that I am so au fait with modern methods; I refrain from telling him that the wall chart was a common method for teaching history when I was at training college twenty years ago.

Soon after this incident we have a new headmaster. Mr Moore is a very reticent man who observes much and says little. During the many years I work with him in charge he gains the respect and affection of all his staff. With degrees in science and mathematics it might seem he would be far removed from primary pupils and their teachers who, in common, have no particular interest in his favourite subjects. The reverse is true. He takes great interest in all subjects at primary level and in a school of over five hundred pupils he knows every child by name.

In these years when we mostly follow set schemes of work he asks us to submit a forecast of steps in each subject which we hope to complete during the coming month. He obviously commits these to memory as, a few days after our forecast books are returned to us, he may drop in to any lesson and know exactly which step he may expect the pupils to have reached in that topic. To take one instance, the teaching of vulgar fractions may take many weeks to pursue and some classes are slower than others. On his occasional visit he grasps quickly the stage the pupils have reached and with blackboard and chalk is unable to resist taking the class on to the next step with all the pupil participation and excitement this provokes. The teacher may feel slightly disappointed that this has been taken out of her hands when she has done the hard slog that precedes it, but Mr Moore does it so graciously that she feels no rancour towards him. There is the odd time when he shares his interest in astronomy with classes and his enthusiasm for the subject, if not the subject itself, claims their full attention, a case of the singer rather than the song. Mr Moore once remarks that he greatly looks forward to reading my monthly forecast which, compared with those of other teachers, gives such detail and according to him makes interesting reading. I, in my turn, find his appreciation an ample reward for the time I spend in forecast preparation.

He is in his middle fifties when he becomes our head and stays with us until he is forced to retire at sixty five. He is a life-long bachelor, living very simply with his unmarried sister and acting as treasurer to his local church. My husband and I find we are fellow guests with him and his sister at a social function held in Glasgow city chambers. As Miss Moore is introduced to us it is she who recognises my husband as a former member of the Sunday-school class she taught thirty five years ago.

Yet another feature of Mr Moore is that he never feels the cold. Our school was built in 1908 and has a heating system which I suspect has not been upgraded since that date. Some wintry mornings we enter a building which is struggling to maintain a temperature above freezing. Teachers and pupils keep their coats and scarves on and hope the radiators may heat up. The headmaster tours the classrooms, checking the radiators at each visit. As the classroom thermometer creeps up to forty-five degrees and he has paid due attention to the teacher's protests that she cannot feel her feet and is likely to suffer a worsening of her chilblains and the children's hands are so cold that they cannot hold their pencils, he takes another look at the thermometer and his comment is, "But it is beginning to heat up." I say, "It could be that the rise in room temperature is the result of the heat loss from the bodies within it." He smiles indulgently and suggests that every half hour or so we abandon the lesson in favour of a five-minute physical exercise session and with that he leaves the room. There are times when he allows us to close the school at midday and the children are sent home with notes of apology to parents while he stays on until four o'clock to supervise the remnant whose parents will not be at home. There are other times when, despite the conditions, he insists that classes continue through the day and I wonder whether, unlike me, he is protected by thermal long johns.

He prides himself on having good judgement and being fair, and in situations where the need for these qualities arises he is firm in his decisions. There is one year of extreme staff shortage when, instead of taking my primary four up to fifth year, I am needed to receive the upcoming third year. He decides that my fourth year class must be split, with half of them going back to another teacher to form a composite class with her fourth year, and the other half going forward to form a composite class with a primary six. I cannot prevent the split but I do question the way he intends to split the class according to age. We have just completed the June examinations which are regularly conducted as the school year is about to close and, if split entirely on age, one of the joint top pupils will go down and the other will go up. I beg him to consider splitting the class according to ability, as in this way the less able pupils will be encouraged by working with the lower standard of work, while the more apt pupils will not be stressed working at a higher level. To my suggestion there is a firm no, on the grounds that the only way he can, to the parents, justify the split is on pupil age. With hindsight I can now better see his reasoning.

In Limewood we have one or two male teachers well outnumbered by the female members of staff. As the seventies progress so does the shortage of teachers and our headmaster keeps a register of retired teachers on whom he may call to man classes for emergency days, weeks or months. For the first time our numbers include several willing to work part-time, so perhaps Glasgow schools are pioneers in adopting time-sharing posts.

I can think of no occasion when our headmaster becomes other than the perfect gentleman. If he is seeking out a lady teacher and is ultimately to find her correcting work on her own in the staffroom, having knocked, he will carefully and intentionally leave the door ajar until the end of the interview allows his departure. I never hear him utter a cross word or show other than equanimity in any situation and we mourn his departure. His sixty-fifth birthday falls on August 23rd and were it to fall just one day later regulations would allow him to continue in his headship. He is sad to have to leave and, as he discovers that my birthday is August 24th, he admits that he wishes we could exchange birthdays.

The headmistress who replaces him spends only her final year with us before she too retires so, in a space of two years, we have three headteachers and as a staff survive many changes.

In the years that I stay at Limewood many changes take place which I can best sum up by reproducing an article I was invited to write for a teacher in-service quarterly publication called *Gleam*.

And the Walls Came Tumbling Down

The phone call from Bath Street ended like this:

"So, I take it you will write something from the angle of the primary teacher?"

"I'll try."

"From your own school situation?"

"If that's what you want."

"Is it open plan, by any chance?"

"No, but I could say something about open minds."

"Just you do that."

A few more details about length and deadline and I went back to my class.

Some minutes later I was reading to my new Primary 4 some stories which last year's Primary 4 wrote in their class Picture Story Book. I was reading one child's version of the visit of Joshua's spies. Strange that when I tell that story, nobody ever seems to think of Rahab as the traitor; quite the reverse — she's a bit of a heroine! I wonder if she herself felt a bit unsure of her loyalties. Writing this I feel much as Rahab might have done, for you see I am a Sassenach and just now I am conscious that the walls have begun to crumble in my Jericho.

I came to Glasgow from Liverpool, where I had been very happy, thinking myself a big fish in a little pond. The little pond was a Primary Girls' School — a tin and timber building left over from World War I, where a fire during one of the summer holidays had put paid to two of our classrooms and the staff-room. So two classes were housed in the boys' department across a main road and a five minute walk away. That was how it all began. The headmaster of the boys' department allowed us to use his hall for drama and dancing on condition that his boys shared our teaching "talent". He threw in the free use of his specialist music teacher. Before long both departments were combining in dramatic projects and for these we shared ideas to make up related schemes of work and revised time tables. We literally took down the curricular walls.

By contrast, when I came to teach in Glasgow I felt surrounded by barriers. I tried to tell the story of Bannockburn without revealing that my sympathies were with the enemy. I switched on to the radio programme, "Exploring Scotland" and couldn't even understand half the language. Marriage and being a "mum" came to my rescue and I did not return to teaching for six years.

It was 1961 when I went back on a temporary, full time basis, just a little better equipped. I couldn't have timed it better.

"You talk like the Beatles, Miss!"

I was accepted. I acquainted myself with the standard text books, I learned what the "Janny" was permitted to do and not do. I discovered that exercise books were "jotters", that cupboards were "presses", pans were "pots", thick in the head was "glaikit", and "flitting" was the chaos before every summer holiday.

I admitted that, compared with the Liverpool schools I knew, the Glasgow schools had better readers and better spellers and, although I still hear Scots talking about the Scottish child being more reticent than his English neighbour, I insist that I have yet to enter the Scottish staff-room where there is any evidence of this hangover into adult life.

The biggest change in children which seemed to have emerged in my six-year absence was that it was no longer as easy to secure their listening attention even with a story and I found myself emulating the students and spending every spare minute making visual aids. Then a television set was installed and to me this was the first breakthrough. It was a breakthrough chiefly because the time-table had to be adapted to allow viewing time as well as PE time, and so a teacher no longer had to feel guilty because her class were doing their sums between 11.00 and 12.00 instead of between 9.30 and 10.30.

Soon after that the phrase "doing their sums" itself took on a new meaning, as teachers were urged to encourage their charges to see more and more ways of doing a calculation. Along with the new understanding came the new child language, and I treasure one reply that came my way when I asked my class to estimate the height of the classroom.

"I guessed you were just a bit taller than Davy Jones, the smallest of the Monkees, so I guessed you were five foot three inches. I stood you on your head three times and you nearly reached the ceiling, so I think that the classroom is about twenty one feet high" . . . part of the pop scene once again.

With a more elastic timetable and more opportunity to correlate subjects came a chance to try out the history "patches" and a necessity for working in groups to share the limited source material. Better still, as Yuri Gagarin became a household word and the Space Man of the comics became a reality, here as it were was the Ark in our midst, the focal point of a tremendous excitement and a proof that history was in the making.

Then came the first blast of the horns! ETV (closed circuit television programmes produced for Glasgow schools) was born and Glasgow really began to communicate with teachers. To switch the image for a moment, we couldn't all be the Mohammeds who found it possible to attend the Saturday, evening and holiday courses through which teachers might keep up with new ideas, but here was ETV bringing the mountain to us. Remember the Cuisenaire (for some time hailed as an original method of introducing children to number through rods of varying size and colour), one of the first of many valuable in-service courses, and invitations to ordinary teachers to help script and relay TV programmes and provide teachers' notes.

Then the final shout — the maths courses for primary teachers and the opportunity to share so many teaching problems, not only those confined to maths. Meantime there was the steady influx into the schools of all the concrete apparatus, the wonderful new books to stimulate free expression in language and such things as the SRA reading kits which finally free the teacher to teach. As I write this with all the parcels arriving daily, one of our auxiliaries says, "It's just like Christmas". The walls have truly begun to shake.

Like many teachers in my age group I'm more than a little frightened by it all. I qualified in the post-war 1940s when every piece of drawing paper was counted out and we had "to make the jotters last" and too frequently school was in one pocket and life in the other. We find it difficult to adjust.

Then, last year, my colleague in the adjoining class, two years out of training college and tuned in to all the new approaches, combined with me in sharing ideas and resources. A cloakroom stands between our two classrooms but there is a communicating door thoughtfully provided by the new fire precautions. We discovered one day that I was older than her mother, but what a great deal I learned from her!

Open Plan? No, we are not Open Plan. We still have walls round the classrooms but buildings are optional barriers. In Liverpool, our members of staff got their best ideas perched on the children's wash-basins drinking their interval tea. I think I realised then that most of the fun in teaching comes from a willingness to be a learner and symbolically the letter on the L-plate is red. Perhaps that is why I am content to be cast as a Rahab and like her to put my faith in a scarlet thread as the walls come tumbling down.

As a result of this article I receive a letter from the Glasgow director of education, in which he states that in the general stuffiness of the material regularly submitted to this publication he found my contribution came like a breath of fresh air and he suggests that I attend his office so he may meet me. At this interview he asks me if I have ever considered writing scripts for school text books, and urges me to attempt this and allow him to pass an opinion on the result. He talks for some time about sentence length, limited vocabulary and optional topics. When I present him with a first draft of my effort, set in the world of middle-class values with which I am familiar, he questions my awareness of the rising numbers of socially deprived and single parent families plus the increasing ethnic minority who now live in Glasgow, and how school text books must change to accommodate all the variations in society. He points out the many instances where my writing does not measure up to this criterion.

Because of his interest in what he kindly calls my talent I meet two or three times with a member of one of the editing teams at Oxford University Press. He is anxious to produce a kit similar to the SRA reading kits which are becoming available to schools. This reading kit consists of short extracts at progressive levels, where the score obtained by answering the written questions at the end of each extract determines the level at which the child proceeds. It is popular with the bright children, who enjoy marking their own work plus the immediate reward of improving their reading skills, and it is popular with teachers as it frees them to give their attention to the less able readers who need their help.

I spend many leisure hours over several months working on a kit to enable children to develop dictionary skills as an aid to spelling and vocabulary and all related to topics of interest. At each stage it receives approval but, as the Thatcher years cut school budgets and the cost of producing the kit soars with inflation, the editors decide that schools will choose to spend their money on essential text books rather than some new, untested and expensive kit. The project is abandoned and, with apologies, I receive a token fee of forty pounds.

It would be a fortunate teacher who among the many classes she receives each year does not at some time find some more difficult than others.

I have to cope with one such class while I am at Limewood. The teacher who passes them on to me does so with these words, "There's a large tail to this class; about a quarter of the pupils have made very little progress in the year that they were with me. The girls are placid enough, content to sit and dream and let everything that we do pass over their heads. The boys are a problem."

Through the year which follows I find that similarly I fail with four of the boys.

Colin is a bright little boy of eight who lives in the tenements opposite the school. Both his parents have jobs. His mother is a school cleaner who is out of the house some hours before he leaves for school and he goes home to an empty house because she begins her work after four o'clock. He is an only child, spending hours of his time alone with no-one to talk to. He makes up for this in school. He cannot stop talking. He talks constantly to his neighbouring pupils, he conducts a running commentary on our activities and, when he is supposed to be concentrating on his own written work, he talks aloud to himself. I try in various ways to get Colin to quieten down, including trying to ignore the distraction but I do not succeed and Colin learns little.

David is plagued by a persistent problem. It occupies all his thoughts and obscures everything else. David lives with his grandmother. It is she who tells me his story. She adopted him when his young parents separated, his father disappeared from his life and his mother left Glasgow to earn a living elsewhere. The grandmother even adopted a younger boy to keep him company. Now his mother, in America, is about to re-marry and wants to have David to live with her. David is convinced that he must choose between staying with the grandmother or going to live in America with the mother he doesn't remember.

I say, "But a little boy of eight cannot be burdened by such a choice."

"We do realise that. The choice has already been made. He is going to his mother. It is David who persists in thinking that he has to make the choice."

It is hardly surprising that the school curriculum seems like trivia to David and I fail to get beyond the blockage.

Billy lives close to my home. He was a late baby in a family with a young mother, a much older father who is a bank manager, and two elder siblings. Because they are neighbours I know that the father demands much in the way of behaviour and achievement from his children. He is prepared to enforce his standards with the strap. The young teenage son has left home and both Billy and his sister stammer very badly. Billy doesn't know how to respond to anything but a very harsh discipline. He has poor attention span and his behaviour is erratic. His work suffers. As in most Glasgow schools the teachers must, at the end of each school year, fill in a printed report card to record test marks with the teacher's comments on each subject. There is a space at the bottom of the card for the teacher to fill in a general comment on attitude to work and general behaviour. On Billy's report card I write "unstable". I choose the word carefully to suggest that he lacks control.

His mother goes to my headmaster to demand that this word be changed. It seems that his father thinks the word "unstable" casts doubt on his son's brain condition. Billy's mother explains what a difficult year this has been at home. Among other strains, Billy's grandfather with whom he had a very loving relationship has died. In trying to be a kind daughter to her surviving mother she has probably neglected Billy.

I say how sorry I am that this has happened and add "It has been a less than normal year for you."

His mother says, "Yes. It has. A great deal of stress"

"And this has affected Billy?"

"It has."

"Then why can you not see that in writing this on his report card, I am only calling your attention to the effect this is having on him in school? You have explained the cause. I am recording the result."

"I do accept your explanation but I know that unless I go home with the word changed my husband is going to blame me."

"I'll make out a new report and substitute a different word but we both know that what I have already written is a true comment."

George, aged ten, ought to be in a class of his age group but because he is still trying to cope with learning to read, he is with me and all my eight-year olds. He has an eye condition which hampers his reading and does not improve his bedraggled appearance. He appears cross-eyed.

Because he is almost illiterate the simplest material that we read together is folk and fairy tale. We read a story in which the hero kills a wolf and George casually tells me that he also has killed a wolf. We read *The Sleeping Beauty* and George tells me that he may have been christened but his mother was not present because he has never had a mother. I cannot help thinking that had there ever been a christening for George, and fairies been invited, they had certainly attended empty-handed. I never meet any member of George's family and in school the other children shun his company. He is often as unwashed as are his smelly clothes.

George cannot cope with a written intelligence test but out of interest I read it aloud to him question by question. One of these requires the child to indicate the odd word in a group. The words are TRUTH, BEAUTY, JUDGE, MERCY, LOVE, four of them qualities which I much doubt he will recognise.

George correctly identifies JUDGE as the odd word. I think this is a lucky guess and press further with "Why?"

"Well", he replies, "A judge is a man and the others . . ." He pauses, stretching his arms wide to demonstrate. "They are all the things which are given to you."

It seems to me that here is George, deprived, as I suspect, of any of the gifts he recognises, expressing a wonder and a gratitude that they exist elsewhere.

Children are unaware how much we, as teachers, learn from them.

The friends I make over the fourteen years that I teach in Limewood are still my friends thirty years later. We frequently meet for lunch and chat and, together, we recall many of our colleagues. It might become apparent to an observer that the skills we used as teachers have somewhat diminished with the passing years as we struggle to remember the names of these colleagues, while the division by three of the lunch plus tip total, once a feat of mental arithmetic we expected from our eight-year-olds, now, for us, demands pencil and paper.

CHAPTER
SEVEN

Even in the best of situations one can become stale and I decide that I need to accept a new challenge in the form of promotion to an assistant headship. For this I am interviewed by a panel composed of some representative from the Education Authority, a Glasgow councillor and a promoted teacher.

Among the panel at my interview I recognise one of the former bridge players at David McLeod School. Perhaps after twenty years she also recognises me, but whether or not she does, I answer truthfully the questions which are put to me from her and the others and, as a result, I am later informed that I am to take up an appointment as assistant head at a school on the south side of Glasgow which is easy to reach from my home. As the Autumn term is about to begin, I receive word to say my appointment has been changed to a school for which I have to travel on both train and bus. I am to occupy this post from October.

I fear that no matter what length of time elapses, I shall never be able to write objectively about the school where I suffer for less than a year in a promoted post. Was it an ancient Pharaoh who believed that if his name were inscribed in stone it was a guarantee that he would be forever remembered?

My name is Ozymandias, king of kings;
Look on my works, ye Mighty, and despair!

I do not want to remember my time at this school and perhaps if I do not record its name my own despair will one day sink into oblivion.

I arrive full of confidence to meet Miss Robb, a headmistress of the "old school" so like the Miss G. of my first school that I am immediately made to feel like a probationer. Why? I think it is because once again I collide with a judgemental, authoritarian attitude. Miss Robb is planning to retire at Christmas. She is irritated by the inconsideration of my predecessor who has been weak enough to succumb to a nervous breakdown after one year in the post. In her first conversation with me she frequently alludes to the incompetence and short-comings of this predecessor as if I were in part responsible for the result.

I am introduced to the promoted teacher in charge of the three infant classes and I meet the teachers of the classes from primary 4 upwards who will be in my department. There are three primary 7 classes at the top of the school. I will teach one of these together with a part-time teacher who comes in three mornings a week to allow me time for administrative work. It does not take long for me to realise that there is no teacher in this school who would not prefer to be somewhere else. They complain about the pupils, their parents, the poor supply of resources, their colleagues, their own home lives but most of all about the way they are treated by the headmistress.

I discover that the person, next to the headmistress, who wields most authority in the school is the janitor, who seems to dictate all the rules. In the evenings certain classrooms are "let" to various social groups in the district. For supervision of these he receives overtime pay. It would appear he spends little of his time in supervision, as in our absence various items are misused or disappear altogether. For this he denies all responsibility. This school is close to the Rangers Football Headquarters and the janitor is an avid supporter of Rangers. The boys need little encouragement to align themselves with him and he with them in all their misdeeds. These include nightly forays to cause damage to the windows of the neighbouring Catholic school. Brought up in the Glasgow culture, "Catholic" for our boys is synonymous with "Celtic". The Catholic boys retaliate so there are few mornings when one or more of our classrooms is not "unsafe for use" and we are forced to "double up" classes.

The primary 7 classes have been arranged not in any order of merit or age but deliberately to break up gangs. The top group in my class are delightful, interested, willing and hard-working but made unhappy by the class trouble-makers, chief of whom is Barry whom they fear. Barry resents the enforced separation from the rest of his cronies who, housed in the parallel classes, he sees only at playtime and after school. He is not at all interested in what goes on in the classroom, except to the extent that he can disrupt the lessons. He is wilful, impudent and vengeful.

I inherit a paper-pellet chucking situation. Bits of paper are screwed up, dipped in the inkwell and fired off the end of a ruler. I never see the first pellet. I do see the one sent in retaliation. The sender of the second pellet always makes the excuse that he was targeted but when I ask by whom he refuses to say. Always the wrong person takes the punishment. In private the pupils tell me that they are warned by their parents never to get on the wrong side of Barry because if provoked he will not hesitate to visit with his gang and vandalise their homes.

Miss Robb treats all her staff, myself included, as puppets to do her bidding. She tells tales about each in turn. According to these tales one is incompetent and lazy, just sitting out the months until she retires. Two others are widowed with young sons to support. Of these one is the assistant head in charge of the three infant classes and the other is always taking time off on supposedly sick leave. Yet another is separated from her husband and is in the throes of divorce proceedings. Mrs. Simon has an invalid husband.

Miss Robb does know the children. Their brothers and sisters have passed through her hands so she knows most of the family histories. She can tell me which members of my class have fathers serving time in Barlinnie jail, others whose fathers are now released and others with brothers who ought to be in prison if the police were doing their job properly.

Because Miss Robb is to retire at the end of the term it is unlikely that much is going to change while I am working with her. I do try to work with her but she is regularly scathing of each effort I make. I am sure that under her headship this has been a good school in the past but she is frustrated by the deterioration in the district and the inability of the incoming population to exercise parental control of their offspring, and is very dissatisfied with her staff. Any suggestions I make to improve their conditions is met with her contempt. She values one or two of her teachers but even they never risk her displeasure by refusing to comply with her demands, despite their inner resentment. Everything is very regimented, including the weekly assemblies where she is likely to publicly upbraid a teacher for failing to control some member of her class.

I suggest to the teachers that they might wish to combine with me in producing a nativity play for the end of term, but they tell me that Miss Robb insists that each class practise a carol of her choice to present at an occasion where she will announce her approval or disapproval of each performance in turn. I decide that I will do the play and accompanying carols with my own class.

My class are used to very formal work so, because I chiefly teach them in afternoon sessions, I hope to introduce less formal teaching. I use a whole afternoon to involve all in creating a colourful history frieze to brighten the classroom with their own work. It survives for just one day. I come into the classroom after the weekend to find it wrecked. I never discover who perpetrated the offence. Because most of my pupils will be entering secondary school at the end of the school year I encourage them to choose their own topic of study, to use the books in the class library to do their own research and to produce some record of their work in personal folders or notebooks. In this way I hope to cultivate their personal interests and it seems that working individually could best cater for a class which at the top end has some very able children and at the bottom end some who are almost illiterate.

There is a pleasant over-burdened secretary who is on the run most of the day in answer to the headmistress's bell. She is often sent to supervise my class so that I too may do Miss Robb's bidding. She is frequently obliged to do the rounds of the classes to inform teachers that there will be no interval as it is too wet for the children to be in the playground. In most schools this is an opportunity for children to learn that the teacher trusts them to behave in her ten minute absence but in this school it seems that training children to exercise self-discipline is not part of the remit.

An evening outing to the pantomime is to prove beyond all doubt that our pupils can behave like uncaged animals. The trip is organised so the teachers are accompanying their classes on a bus hired for the occasion. I am prepared for the children being noisy and singing songs en route. I am not prepared for their pushing and shoving and refusal to stay in their seats, a behaviour which is going to irritate the driver and threaten the safety of all concerned. Miss Robb with her friend meets us at the theatre. They choose to sit quite apart from us. She complains bitterly about everything, the seat of her own choosing, the behaviour of the children, the inability of the staff to control them and for the fact that we are turned out of the foyer to wait in the rain for the buses which are late in arriving to take us back to the school. For the next weeks I am left in no doubt that I am to blame for all these things. I am beginning to discover that Miss Robb obtains much pleasure from making her underlings feel inadequate.

Miss Robb often leaves school after the interval on Friday afternoons. This particular Friday she informs me that she is allowing the other two primary 7 teachers to leave with her. I end up with over a hundred children sitting in my room, three to a desk with some on the floor at the front. This situation is so similar to the one at Wavertree in Liverpool that I need hardly detail the order of events. Barry has the comradeship of all his gang and is out to impress them with his ability to create mayhem. He shoots the first pellet, only this time I see him. I am determined that all present are going to witness him being punished. I haul him out to the front of the class but he refuses to take the strap. I push him out of the classroom and into my workroom next door. There he picks up the chair and holds it above his head as a weapon. It becomes clear to me that he is going to use this chair if I have the temerity to approach him. Instinct tells me that he cannot hold the chair above his head indefinitely. The moment arrives when his arms drop and I use the strap. This time I do not miss and his screams of rage precede us as I push him back into the classroom for all to witness the mighty fallen. Barry, undefeated, throws open the lid of the desk and flings the contents at me. I tell him that he is to remain behind after school is dismissed. Within minutes the four o'clock bell rings, and although I attempt to make the class file out in some order, Barry's cronies mill round him forming a bodyguard to ensure his escape.

I am shattered. There is no-one in the building to whom I can report the incident. I go home, ring a Glasgow inspector who knows me personally and ask his advice. He tells me to record the whole incident in writing and to refuse to have Barry in my class at any time in the future. On Monday I am to ask my headmistress to endorse my statement before posting it into the Glasgow Education Office.

I follow his advice but Miss Robb refuses to have any part in demanding Barry's exclusion. She tells me that when her professional career is so near its close, she certainly does not wish to leave with a blemish on her headship. She adds that I am not the first teacher in a city school to be so threatened by a pupil. It is an everyday occurrence and I must have led a very sheltered life not to have come across this kind of happening elsewhere. For me to send off my report will only reveal my own incompetence and damage my future in teaching. I tell her this is no threat to me. All my life I have taught because I chose to, not because I had to. Fortunately I have a husband who earns a wage that will support the two of us and so I am free to do as

I have been advised and, with or without her consent, I am posting the report. Not only do I post the report but I also compose my resignation from this appointment. With the notice I am required to give, this will become effective at the end of the summer term.

From that day on Miss Robb makes my life as miserable as she can but my letter secures Barry's exclusion from the school and there is but a very short time to the Christmas holiday, a time both assistant headteachers have to unwillingly spend making arrangements for Miss Robb's retirement dinner. Most of the staff are disinclined to attend the function and loath to contribute towards a retirement present. Miss Robb presents us with a list of ex-colleagues she wishes to include in the invitations. We know to expect the presence of some office dignitary. As a staff we are required to cover the whole cost and it is my fellow senior member of staff and I who have to compensate for our reluctant staff by increasing our own unwilling contributions.

On the final day of the term Miss Robb comes into my room to deliver her parting shot. "I hope that at some time in the future you may become a good assistant head teacher. You may even achieve the necessary competence to stage a school play."

I vainly hope that Miss Robb will be replaced by some awe-inspiring male who might ensure a climate in which we could teach.

Miss Digby, the lady who is appointed to the headship, is small in stature and has only ever taught in an infant department. She is happy to be involved with the three youngest classes but is hesitant to cross the threshold of any classroom with pupils over the age of seven. While she and the infant mistress deal between them with three infant classes I am expected to cope with the other six.

Coping with the other six requires me to be responsible for the schemes of work, allocation of resources, requisitioning new materials and reorganisation of classes when teachers are absent. I plan projects for my own pupils but again and again circumstances crop up which forces them to be shelved or abandoned. I bitterly resent the time I have wasted in planning these projects.

Miss Digby's method of dealing with badly behaved pupils is to have them report to her as each day begins. The offenders form a long queue where they can happily waste the waiting time as each in turn is admonished. This appears to have little effect on them as they constantly re-offend. Their frustrated class teachers take what they consider more immediate and appropriate action, so at intervals during the day I am faced with pupils saying that they have been sent to me to be strapped.

Yet another way in which I am interrupted is when Miss Digby requests my presence to play co-hostess to the police. Because of the ongoing vandalism in the area the police become regular callers. I resent the time I have to spend drinking tea with the police. I haven't spent all these years in teaching to end up doing this.

We have a young school chaplain who has realised that in this school the staff are in greater need of his ministrations than are the children. With our classes we are invited to attend his church for the Easter service. A day or two before the service is due to take place Miss Digby asks me to visit the Manse to hand in the order of service she has arranged. In it are the hymns and readings she has selected. I attempt to suggest that usually the selection is left to the chaplain. Alternatively she could invite him so that they might together discuss the matter. She says she prefers me to deliver her choice so I become the embarrassed messenger.

From time to time I am approached by the headmistress to accept Barry back into my class. It seems that the parents, police and Education Office all pester her regularly. It is legally his right to receive education and with his additional leisure he has become a nuisance to the local shopkeepers. It is not possible for him to be indefinitely excluded. To these pleas I suggest that another school could be asked to accept him but apparently his infamy has spread beyond the district and no other school is willing to put up with him.

"So you see," concludes Miss Digby, "We are left with no choice. We must take him back."

"Not in my class." I say and I warn the other teachers to similarly refuse.

Finally I am asked. "If he is allowed to work under supervision in another room, are you willing to set and mark the work he does?"

To this I agree. It is only a matter of weeks before Barry is due to be moved to a secondary school.

As we progress through the summer term there are several events to be planned. I have to draw up the arrangements and submit them for Miss Digby's approval. The first of these is a sports day, the second an outing to Edinburgh Zoo for the children who will be leaving primary at the end of June. These pupils have been invited to visit their secondary school so another afternoon they have to be escorted there. At some time I must take stock of all the needlework and handwork materials as the stock book is periodically to be produced for external inspection. Finally, the practice of awarding a Dux prize, which has prevailed here during Miss Robb's jurisdiction, is to be continued so I am asked to draw up the test paper.

To this last request I vehemently protest. I am one of the three primary 7 teachers. I can only base this test on work covered by my pupils, which must be seen by the other primary 7 teachers to favour the contestants from my class. I beg that she prepare the test paper or at least compile it from suggestions made by all three class teachers. When she refuses I am well aware that it is because she has no idea of anything taught above the level of primary 4.

One Monday morning a set of questionnaires are delivered from the Bath Street office. Each teacher must fill in the number of hours she spends with her pupils for each day in the current week. I pass my completed form to the headmistress. She is horrified. She explains to me that the information we give is intended to reflect what is scheduled in a normal week, while this week Mrs. Simon was absent and there were two mornings when two classroom windows were being repaired and so the timetable had to be rearranged. I point out the underlined statement at the top of the form where it is indicated that we are to record the current week.

"Ah, yes. But not if it were such a week as it was."

"Then perhaps you would like to re-write my entry because I will not. It is only right that whoever is collecting this information be made aware that in this school this is the norm not the exception."

The general behaviour of the pupils is not improving so the headmistress is now referring certain pupils to the Educational Psychologist. One particular child so referred visits the boys' toilet washrooms before school begins and uses the washbasin for his excretions. Frequently as I set foot in the building the janitor insists on my accompanying him to view what he calls "fresh evidence".

Perhaps it is not surprising that trying to develop strategies to overcome my inadequacy I stay up until the early hours and my sleep is disturbed by unpleasant dreams. The over-acidic stomach which I seem to have acquired is causing me pain.

My journey home in the late afternoon involves a connection with an infrequent train service. It is an electric line, beset by occasional flooding. The train doors vary from refusing to open at the stations to refusing to close when we are ready to depart, causing long delays. It is often but minutes to six o'clock when I reach home. There is no time to relax with a tea or coffee before I must at least have the meal on the way for my husband coming in from his job. I do consider boosting my spirits with a quick sherry but remind myself of the screen injunction at the end of the film *The Days of Wine and Roses* to "never drink in need". The policeman who lives next door has for about six months been on sick leave with a nervous breakdown. Through the wall I hear him singing. He seems to be happy living in an economy which allows him to enjoy life on the taxes I am paying.

"Why am I working in such an unhappy situation to keep him in comfort?" I ask my doctor this question when eventually I have to visit her surgery. Her reply, "There are two kinds of people in this world. One kind is prepared to do as little as they can and the rest like you and me have to work twice as hard to support them. You have to decide which set you want to belong to."

She gives me a renewed prescription for Valium but she also gives me a medical certificate which allows me a week's respite from school.

I suffer not a qualm of conscience that this means my colleagues must, without me, undertake the outing to Edinburgh Zoo. They tell me afterwards how some of the pupils, enjoying the freedom afforded by the unrestricted conditions, caused them more than a little concern, especially when in trying to round them up for the return journey they were delayed for another hour. It is a repetition of our outing to the pantomime, only this time there is no Miss Robb to lay the blame on me. When, at the end of the week, I re-visit the surgery the doctor provides me with a strategy to get through the rest of the summer term. "When someone makes excessive demands on your time, I think you will find it works to just say 'No'. Don't attempt to give explanations or excuses, say 'No' and nothing else. You'll find there's little they can say or do."

The over-burdened secretary greets me on my return and I share with her the wise words of the doctor. Later that morning I am able to tell her how successfully the strategy functions.

Miss Digby says, "While you were off school did you manage to prepare the Dux examination?"

" No."

"So, you'll find time to do that today?"

"No."

"Well, you will have to find time to go into town this afternoon and select and order all the new books for the library."

"No."

The sky does not fall on my head and my spirits revive.

For the rest of the time I am at this school I tell myself that for whatever administrative job I leave incomplete or badly done, I will not be around to suffer the consequence. I throw all the official forms I have never had time to attend to into the waste bin. I check the needlework and handwork stock books, fail to make them tally and leave them to tell their own tale. To the rest of the staff I bestow all the pictures and teaching aids I have collected over the years. In return they give me a present of cash which I spend at a craft shop. I buy designs and materials to keep me busy for a long time in occupational self-therapy.

Partly to compensate my colleagues for my failure in my post and partly because it gives me great satisfaction, I commit a sin which if or when it is ever discovered it will be too late to affect its intended result.

I am supposed to draw up the list of pupils for transfer to secondary school, strictly according to age. When I go through the register lists I ignore the discrepancy of months which could exclude most of the trouble makers. I decide that these children will benefit from an extra few months under the rule of a larger and, I hope, firmer staff in a secondary school and I add their names to the list. I hope that even without me this school will get a fresh start and that in my place they appoint someone who has behind him some experience in the police force or prison reform. There is no Dux examination. On my last day the pain in my back is so severe that I take a taxi home.

I regret that at the end of this odyssey there is no child to remember with affection. It is a cause of sorrow to me that I never had time to really get to know the children in my class. I am conscious only of my failure. I failed from the moment I applied for promotion. I failed to appreciate that I did not have the qualities required. I thought age and experience and an enthusiasm to share ideas with other teachers, plus a deep desire to take a personal interest in all the children would be enough, but I was wrong. It might have helped if I had been younger so I could have kicked against the injustice as I did in the first school. Then I had the wonderful assurance that I was right. It might have helped if I had not known what it was to work in a happy school. As an assistant teacher there had been time to share interval coffees and lunch breaks and exchange ideas, time which in promotion is taken up elsewhere doing some other part of the job. It certainly could have helped if I had been less vulnerable. I was not prepared for total inadequacy. I never want to teach again.

CHAPTER
EIGHT

For several months I revel in my freedom and quickly heal. I have not had time to become bored when one morning I answer the phone to hear the new headmaster of the local secondary school speaking.

"Mrs Park? I hear from my regular meetings with head-teachers of our local primary schools that you have stopped teaching. Is that correct?"

When I assure him this is so, he goes on, "You know, of course, that we have to provide a common course for first and second year pupils in all subjects. Some of the less able children are rapidly out of their depth. I am looking for a teacher to do remedial work in English and Arithmetic. It would entail working with individuals or small groups, no class teaching. I'm restricted to recruiting a part-time teacher, probably a total of three days each week. How would you feel about that?"

I feel overwhelmed. All the confidence I used to have bounces back.

"When would I start?"

"I'm thinking of after the summer holiday."

"Could I come in after Easter so that I'd have the short summer term to see how it would work?"

"That's fine with me. Would you know how to administer diagnostic tests?"

"Oh, yes," I lie, knowing I can find out before Easter.

"And given time off work, would you be prepared to take a course in remedial training?"

"Certainly, but I've just realised I'll need time off to attend my daughter's wedding down south in May."

"Oh, I think we can give you that. See you after Easter then, and thank you."

Thank ME! I'm thanking whatever gods there are. No class teaching! Just an opportunity to really teach. It is the fulfilment of every teacher's dream.

It is a glorious Spring. I never wear a coat as I walk through the park and up the hill to school through April, May and June. So begins my first term as a lone teacher introducing a remedial department in Kingston. This school has a total roll of one thousand eight hundred pupils, coinciding with the population of the Falklands, on whose behalf we are, at this time, fighting a war. There are eight first year classes.

There is no classroom of even cupboard proportions to permanently house myself and the individuals or groups that, daily, grow larger in numbers. Much as the Israelites did in the wilderness, we wander up and down corridors over five storeys. The promised land that we are hoping to find is a vacant space. There is a limit to the books and equipment that we can carry and of these there are few items adequate to our needs. I quickly adapt to teaching off the top of my head.

As a standby, I am inspired to arm myself with a badly typed, first draft of a story I have written for this

119

age group. I hope that by reading extracts from it I may arouse in my pupils an urge to produce some creative writing.

My remit is to help the less able first and second years cope with their English and Arithmetic, but soon disruptive pupils from all age groups are being sent to me. My haven is fast becoming a sin bin. After half a lifetime in primary teaching, despite my current difficulties, I feel guilty that my present school life seems comparatively so relaxing. I sympathise with the members of staff who beg me to take their troublesome pupils. I have yet to learn to say No.

One of my pupils is Alex. Alex is fifteen. His father is an alcoholic and his mother is in a mental home. To him the school curriculum is so remote that he rarely spares it a second thought. He does enjoy reading and, when I am able to savour the luxury of teaching him as a single pupil, I realise he is an intelligent boy who not only comprehends and sensitively appreciates what he reads but also orally expresses himself well. On occasions, when a time-tabled subject or teacher is not to his liking, he excuses himself from those classes on the grounds that he has to attend remedial tuition. More and more frequently he chooses the soft option of turning up in my class. Thus he is one of a number of pupils in the group who first listen to the opening chapter of my story, *The Magic of the Wild Park*.

As an introduction I tell the children that the story is set in the district adjacent to the school. Some of the characters live in Old Castle Road in the oldest part of Cathcart. The park is the Linn Park with the river running through it. The path, alongside the river, is that same path which many of us tread, daily, on our way to school. I then read from the beginning where one of the four teenagers, Adam, takes shelter in a thunderstorm in the wild section of the park and imaginatively enters a prehistoric time zone to become a cave dweller, called Og.

Some days later I am halfway through a lesson with a small group, trying to give them some understanding of decimal notation, when Alex appears. Accepting my explanation that I can neither include him in the group nor teach him separately in this period, he agrees to choose a book and read.

"Do you have that story here, 'cos then I could find out what happens to that wee fellow, Og?"

Ridiculously, perhaps, I am flattered and away he goes to a corner with the less than pristine manuscript.

From that day on, every time that I cannot manage to fit Alex into the group, he makes the same request and reads for himself how each character in turn enters a different time zone to get under the skin of some long-ago person. At the end of each session Alex lingers behind to ask me questions about the characters or the ideas.

The months pass and the day comes when Alex is leaving school for the last time. He comes to say Goodbye. As he reaches the door he looks back:

"That magic of the wild park, where could I find it?"

I am never to forget Alex and his final question. I am unable to answer it. On the one hand, here is a fifteen-year old boy apparently asking the equivalent of, "Where would I go to find Santa Claus?"

I refuse to believe that Alex is asking the question at this infantile level. Nor is he asking me to direct him through the rusty gate and over the rotting bridge. He could find these for himself. On the other hand, if he is asking, "How can I get into another time; another world to escape my wretchedness? How can I tap into the magic?" I still am unable to answer.

I have yet to find the school or the teacher to provide the magic that Alex is looking for.

I think for me this episode sums up the privileged position I enjoy in this school. It is a unique position in which to teach because the remedial teacher is forced into asking questions of himself and constantly learning.

One group who come to me say, "We all failed the Arithmetic test last term. Nobody can understand what Mr. Singh is saying. There are two of our class who say they can understand him but they didn't pass either."

I try working with workbooks so that each pupil may progress at his own pace. One boy races through the assignments but when I question him I discover that he has little comprehension of any process. I abandon the work books.

Despite the fact that I am only supposed to be teaching Arithmetic, it is hard to resist the children's pleas to help them with their Geometry and Algebra homework. I take home the maths text books to keep a chapter ahead of them with the "New Maths" and I relearn all the Geometry and Algebra that I never understood when I was a pupil at school.

No-one appears to resent giving up lesson time to get help. I tell them that university students attend tutorials so in a similar way, when they are coming to me, it is to get special time on their own. The headmaster is frequently checking up on the children who waste their time on corridors. He thinks it very amusing when one day he nabs what he thinks is one such pupil only to be told, quite defensively and with pride, "I'm going to my tutorial with Mrs. Park."

I spend the last four weeks of the term on the first half of a remedial course. I learn as much from the conversation of other remedial teachers as I do from the psychologists and sociologists who lecture on the course. Students are required to do much reading, essay writing and case studies in their own time and to attend the occasional weekend seminar.

When I return to school after the summer break the new recruits from the nine new first year classes swell the ranks. It is to my long-term advantage when my tutor from the remedial course decides to vet me for a whole day. The headmaster arranges for me to have a room for that day and due to the pleas of my tutor on my behalf it becomes mine for the rest of my days.

"Would you be able to cope with a fourth year girl with dyslexia?" asks the headmaster.

Debbie is very intelligent. I mug up on some of the features of dyslexia and she and I work together on some of her spelling and reading problems. I lend her my own copy of *A Town like Alice* and she says it is one of the few books that she has ever managed to finish.

Robert is a third year dyslexic. He is very keen on conjuring tricks and performs at school concerts. He does not lack confidence but he lacks motivation to tackle his difficulties. I say, "You know, Robert, when you become famous, you will need to keep track of your public engagements and look after your cash account."

He grins at me, "Maybe, but I'll be able to afford a secretary to do that, won't I?"

I think Robert will survive without my assistance. He might not even need a secretary if he buys a computer.

James is more of a challenge. I remember him from primary school although I was never his class teacher. His extremely poor eyesight was diagnosed too late for him to learn basic skills, too late because in order to appear the same as his peers he has become used to disguising his ignorance. He is adept at turning the pages of a book to give the impression that he is reading. By his final year in secondary he decides to attend or not attend lessons as he deems fit. He is only putting in time until he can leave school.

One of the rules of remedial teaching is to find out where a pupil's interest lies and what he already knows, find his strengths and build on them. While other pupils leave school with their satchels full of books, I see James walking home each day uncluttered except for perhaps a single book. When I question him about this he says he goes straight from school to work with a local greengrocer. He hopes this job will continue when he leaves school. I discover also that he attends a local

Boys' Brigade and is saving up to go to camp. This particular B.B. is locally famous for its band in which James plays the drums.

In the staff room one day I casually mention James and his drums. The head of the music department says, "Send James along to me and I'll see if he could possibly join the orchestra for the school concert."

James tells me that, as a result, he has to pay attention to the notice board where the times of orchestra rehearsals will be listed. At last, James has some motivation to learn the rudiments of reading.

I include this story of James because I think that sometimes, when schools fail, it is possible for some influence outside of school life to give a pupil a sense of esteem.

At the end of the school concert this year, the headmaster stands up and gives his vote of thanks to all taking part, mentioning a special few by name. He concludes, "A special thanks to our drummer, James Mackenzie." James receives his own special share of the applause.

Over the years the headmaster increases my stock allowance to cover the cost of reading kits in various forms. One which is very popular with my pupils is a set of short books which have illustrations on every page and, as in comics, the words coming out of the mouths of the characters in bubbles. There is a short text below the picture and this is duplicated on a radio-cassette. Each child is provided with miniature ear-phones so he may listen to the tape as he follows the text.

When a child is sent to me for assessment, he or she will frequently say. "It's not that I can't read. It's just that I make mistakes when I have to read aloud in front of the class."

"That's okay," I say, "I promise you that in this class you will never be asked to read aloud."

It is a rule that when we listen to the tape we must keep our eyes on the text. We are listening to and reading *Oliver Twist* in a much abridged version. At present such tapes are only published by American firms so the story is narrated in an American voice. I'm sure that for my pupils this is a plus factor.

The day arrives when a pupil who has missed a chapter through absence rejoins the group. I say, "Shall we briefly tell Fiona what happened in the part of the story she missed or should I just reread it through for all of us without the tape?"

One child says, "We could take the part of the characters and the storyteller and we could read it to her."

"You mean you want to read it aloud?"

They are all anxious to take part and this they do, reading fluently in AMERICAN accents.

One of the twins who comes to me throughout two years says to me one day, "You taught me to read."

I smile, "I'm not sure how much of that was due to me."

"You did, Miss. It was those tapes. They made it fun."

Subject teachers refer to guidance teachers the pupils who are having difficulties in their classes. Guidance teachers refer them to me. Sometimes subject teachers refer them directly to me. Remedial pupils themselves arrive some days accompanied by a hopeful new recruit who sees my small group as an easy option to a subject he dislikes. I discourage this, saying I can only accept pupils referred by teachers. I do not tell them that I even harbour doubts about the number of pupils sent to me by some subject teachers.

I receive such a bunch of first years from one teacher. I ask these pupils to tell me what they think are the particular obstacles they meet in that class. They tell me that the teacher dictates the notes which they have to take home to learn. They cannot keep up with the pace of his dictation and they cannot make sense of the misspelt, unfinished sentences they have written in their notes.

I go to their subject teacher and ask, "Are there no text books which these pupils could use for their revision homework?" He shows me a beautiful book, the Roman and Greek classic myths with illustrations throughout. He opens a cupboard door to reveal the complete set in mint condition.

"Do you think I would allow pupils to take these books home?"

"Well, could I borrow half a dozen to use with them in my class?"

"Certainly not. These books stay locked in my cupboard. By the way, I'd like to borrow your room to show a film on Thursday. It's the easiest room to black out."

This is the same teacher who, when he was teaching only one sixth year pupil, would not allow me with my pupil to share library space with him during the term before I had a room of my own.

"Sorry," I say, "All my equipment is there and I need different kits for different individuals. You will have to arrange to view the film on one of the days I am not in school."

He does and for some reason he leaves his class unsupervised for a spell. I find all my library books in a muddle and other items disturbed or destroyed. From then on my room is locked in my absence.

Because a small group gives assurance, the children often want to confide in me the difficulties they have with the personalities of some other teachers. I do try to avoid this but I'm tempted to listen because it does have its humorous side.

As if to explain all, one child sums up his complaint with, "You see, Miss, he's English."

I say, "I'm English."

"I know, but you don't talk like him."

With a similar prejudice to that of the child I accept his comment as a compliment. The accent the child dubs as "English" is a southern one. I am from the north.

One young teacher in his first year of teaching is only a colleague of mine for the one term that I am moving round the school with my groups. I sometimes find myself next door to him and he seems to spend all his time using the belt and haranguing in a loud voice. When I meet up with him in a corridor and he complains about his dreadful classes, I mention a couple of alternative methods which he might find helpful. He is obviously not to be persuaded from his own approach. He concludes, "I believe in establishing my authority. Discipline first."

I recall saying almost these identical words many years ago.

When I return to school after the summer holiday, he is no longer on the scene. I ask another young teacher if Mr. Worthing has left. "Gone back to England, I guess," is his reply. "Probably got himself a job as a prison warder."

In this school of four storeys there are about half a dozen staff-rooms. I share the "lower ladies", a title referring to our position on the ground floor rather than our status. From time to time one or two male staff take refuge in our peace and quiet. Ours is a very friendly staff-room, my colleagues, mostly heads of departments, treating me as an equal when in fact I feel a bit of an oddity — the only English teacher, three days a week, primary trained with no degree. Contrary to my experience in primary staff-rooms, school is not the main topic of conversation. These, mostly unmarried, ladies in their fifties talk about theatre, cinema, television programmes and topical news. There is much discussion and much laughter.

I am attending an evening course for remedial teachers. There's a great deal of emphasis on sharing classroom teaching, recording pupil progress, teacher accountability and teacher assessment. It would seem that the practice of withdrawing pupils from classes is to be abandoned. I voice my concern to a fellow member of staff who is also one of the deputy heads. A day or two later she delivers a message from the headmaster, "Tell Mrs. P. from me that she is to carry on in her own way. It suits the pupils and it suits me. If the course is upsetting her tell her to give it up." I do. Only weeks later he tells me that in order to please a higher authority I have to share some of the Maths and English classes with subject teachers.

"How?" I ask.

"Well, I imagine the subject teacher will present the material and for the part of the period when the pupils are doing their own written work, you will be reinforcing the teaching by giving help to the weakest pupils."

"Don't you think the kids will feel even more inadequate, singled out for help in a class situation while still trying to cope with work which is beyond them?"

"I think they probably will but we have to try it."

We try it in Maths. To be fair it does work with a first year class, taken by a young male head of department who, zealous himself, fills his pupils with enthusiasm for the Geometry and Algebra which for them are new subjects and in which they have not yet dropped behind. He and I jointly spend time at the desks of all the pupils.

It is a disaster with a second year class where the teacher is partially deaf and some of the children take advantage of this to keep up a constant chatter while paying little attention to what is being taught. The teacher spends most of her time illustrating her points on the blackboard with her back to the class, unaware of all the inattention. When it is time for the pupils to apply the rule for themselves, most of them sit with raised hands waiting for someone to individually re-affirm the teaching they did not bother to listen to. It is an impossible task.

Mr. Stewart, the head of the English department, is ambitious and dedicated to making the new methods work. Some members of his department are willing to cooperate and so in many of the English classes there is less teacher and more pupil discussion. He prefers to have his own staff doing the remedial work within their own classes, with me continuing to extract the more extreme cases.

We compromise by having fewer shared periods and not removing pupils from Maths or English periods. I reorganise my timetable to accommodate my remedial pupils, to be withdrawn where possible from other subjects of their choice.

Mr. Stewart's criticism of one of my lessons is "Too much teacher". It is true. I want the children to talk and finally write about some idiosyncratic character whom they know. I read them a humorous poem on such a theme. I tell them about my neighbour, Charlie, who spends much of his time sitting behind the wheel of his new car in the garage, as my husband says, "Driving down the M1". For every ten ideas I plant in their heads I am hoping that one might spark off some response in the child. Mr. Stewart suggests I should split my group into smaller groups to talk among themselves about the topic before sharing their findings with the rest. When I try this, I find some groups talking about anything other than the topic while others are picking a quarrel. In the absence of any bright pupils to act as leaders in the groups, it seems to me I have to be the group leader.

By now, the increase in the school roll allows us to recruit an extra teacher. Added to the English department is a teacher specially trained and delegated to deal with pupils for whom English is a second language. These are mostly children of Asian parents who already attend my remedial classes. This teacher shares my small room, so we have to find ways of teaching with the minimum of noise.

No sooner has this teacher been given his own space elsewhere than the headmaster takes on a second remedial teacher who is putting in some months full time before she and her doctor husband embark on missionary work abroad.

The headmaster approaches me with, "How would you like to come in full time to be paid as head of the department?"

My husband has just retired. He is far from well and is less than happy that I am still working even part-time. I explain this to the headmaster and suggest that I can work quite happily with Hazel if, because she is full time, he puts her in charge of the department. He thinks this is a great joke. So Hazel and I work together, with me, supposedly, as her boss, splitting the groups and sharing the room.

The years fly by in this school. The headmaster will retire this summer and so will I. I look back on the various schools in which I have been employed. I am a true Virgo, critical, making snap judgements which I later have to revise. My opinions of schools and certain members of staff have mellowed over the years. With hindsight I can see my own arrogance and intolerance. I can see where I blamed others instead of myself, and if it is still apparent in this record it is because I have tried to recapture how I felt in those situations. Despite the times when I congratulated myself on what I thought my success, I am not at all sure how much I taught. I do know that if I taught nothing, in my final years at Kingswood I certainly learned more than in all the other schools put together.

It is this conclusion which I express in my retirement speech at the end of June 1984, adding how pleasant it has been to work for three bosses, head of Maths, head of English and the retiring headmaster. Such a position enabled me to choose the advice from whichever of the three suited me best at the time.

Magnanimously I praise all the staff for their cooperation, with special reference to three members of staff whom I had some time ago recognised as former pupils of mine. In the long ago days when I taught them, there was on the Glasgow primary timetable a weekly spot devoted to the teaching of "Morals and Manners". From these lessons they must have learned something because, until today, my three former pupils have had the good manners never to mention the fact that I was of such mature vintage to have been their teacher when they were children.

I recall a retirement speech of a former colleague. She said she had become used to new pupils informing her that she had taught one or other of their parents. What concerned her was the possibility that one day soon some pupil would inform her that she had taught his grandparent. It was this concern that prompted her to take her departure from teaching.

Because I continue to live in the area of the schools where I taught, there are still occasions, some twenty years after my retirement, when I discover that the person I am speaking to remembers me as his teacher. I struggle to remember him and sometimes I have to admit defeat.

A few years ago my son and I had to spend time with the local undertaker to make funeral arrangements. It turned out that this not so young undertaker remembered me as the Mrs. Park who had taught him when he was eight years old. He was happy to spend a considerable time reminiscing about other members of his class and other teachers at that school. After about half an hour of this my son and I excused ourselves on the grounds that we had to keep an appointment with the lawyer who also practised locally. As we were about to enter the lawyer's office, my son felt it necessary to give me a word of advice, "Mum, I hope you will forgive my saying this but, should you discover that you taught the lawyer, you will bear in mind that for every five minutes of his time we take it will be added to his fee."

Even an ex-teacher must admit that the learning process does not end with retirement. My children and grandchildren continue to make me aware of all that I have yet to learn.

I Married Joan

Joan Park

Joan Park's affectionate 'autobiography' of her life with her husband, Alex.

"What kind of a wife do you think Joan would make?" This was the start of the marriage between Joan, a teacher from Liverpool, and Alex Park, eleven years her senior and from Glasgow. Married in 1953, Joan moved to Glasgow and into a very different world from the one she had known, for Alex expected a wife who stayed at home, brought up the children and kept a good house. She, an experienced teacher, wished to continue her career.

Joan Park's account of her marriage, as seen through her husband's eyes, is humorous and encouraging, a wonderful glimpse into the hardships of the immediate post-War years through the changes of the 1960s and 1970s to the present.

ISBN 0-7531-9988-2 (hb)
ISBN 0-7531-9989-0 (pb)

86 Smith Street

Park, Joan

A memoir that recaptures ordinary family life in 1930s Britain

Daughter of a ship steward and a housewife, Joan Park gives a delightful glimpse of her childhood from 1927 to 1941, when she and her family lived at 86 Smith Street in Liverpool.

From the descriptions of her granddad's shoe repair shop to the stories her mother used to tell, Joan Park recounts her personal memories of the time of the Great Depression with a child's innocent eye. This is life as she encountered it in those days — family, friends, school and the little incidents — all of which had a big part to play in the day-to-day life of a little girl growing up in Liverpool.

ISBN 0-7531-9842-8 (hb)
ISBN 0-7531-9843-6 (pb)